INSPIRATIONAL BASKETBALL STORIES FOR KIDS

25 LEGENDARY PLAYERS IN THE GREATEST GAMES FROM THE COURT

TY MCDANIEL

Disclaimer

Inspirational Basketball Stories for Kids
First Edition: October 29, 2023
Copyright © 2023 Caliber Brands Inc.

CONTENTS

INTRODUCTION

Hey there, young basketball fans! Prepare to be moved by the NBA's most extraordinary stories. The NBA is more than just a sports league; it represents prestige and distinction in the basketball world. It serves as the pinnacle of achievement for players, coaches, and fans alike, and to be a part of it is a remarkable honor.

Wearing an NBA jersey is a fantasy come true for any aspiring player. It represents the pinnacle of years of dedication, hard work, and passion for the game. Being drafted into the NBA is a significant accomplishment that acknowledges a player's skill and potential in the league. The privilege of representing a team, as well as, a city or state, carries with it an obligation and expectation of excellence.

Players who achieve immortal status are those who confront obstacles, conquer adversity and break records. And these are exactly the kinds of stories you will find in this book.

The players chosen for the pages within were picked based on their record breaking performances and ability to push through adversity during intense moments. They are masters of making critical plays when their team needed them the most.

However, these stories are not just about scoring points or making spectacular plays; they are about perseverance, overcoming adversity, and accomplishing the impossible.

Consider the legendary Michael Jordan. He is renowned for his unwavering determination. However, he was not a basketball titan by chance. He taught us that with diligence and perseverance, it is possible to realize our dreams.

Likewise, the story of LeBron James demonstrates the power of self-confidence. As a child, he began practicing basketball and always believed he could make it to the NBA. By having faith in himself and his abilities, he overcame obstacles and attained extraordinary success.

In the NBA, athletes learn to recover from setbacks. It's important to understand that they do not always succeed, however they do not allow defeats to discourage them. They learn from their mistakes and come back more powerful. It is normal to make mistakes in life—however, what matters most is how we recover and move forward.

Even more importantly, NBA players are renowned for their sportsmanship. They play fairly, respect their opponents, and are excellent sportsmen regardless of the outcome. These stories serve as a reminder that being respectful and kind to others is equally as essential as winning.

Prepare yourselves, young readers, for a journey through the grand tapestry of the NBA, where the stories of its finest players in some of their best moments are more than just tales of basketball greatness— they are life lessons. And just like the NBA heroes you will soon discover, you have the ability to overcome obstacles and claim your own slam dunk to victory!

1

MICHAEL JORDAN - GAME 6 OF THE 1998 NBA FINALS

In June of 1998, the NBA championship was at stake in the world of basketball as all eyes were glued on one game. Michael Jordan, the legendary player for the Chicago Bulls, was leading his team against the Utah Jazz. The Bulls led the series 3-2, and this was Game 6; a victory here would crown the Bulls champions.

Both teams had given their all throughout the game. With only seconds remaining on the clock, the Bulls trailed by one point. The arena was rife with anticipation and tension. The championship's outcome hung in the balance.

Frequently referred to as the "Greatest Basketball Player of All Time", Michael Jeffrey Jordan was born in Brooklyn, New York, on February 17, 1963. From an early age, he had a passion for sports, particularly basketball. He was a talented athlete who also understood the value of a strong work ethic.

He had always loved basketball, and he wanted to compete for the Emsley A. Laney High School varsity team. However, something unexpected occurred when he was a sophomore – he did not make the cut.

Can you imagine his disappointment? It was a situation that could have deterred others, but not Michael. He did not surrender. Instead, he made a decision that would alter his life's path. He resolved to work even harder in order to prove his worth and demonstrate to everyone that he belonged on the varsity team.

The setback did not paralyze him; he used it as motivation. He spent hours every day after school honing his shots, dribbles, and maneuvers on the basketball court. He would fire until the sun set, and sometimes even under the light of the streetlamps. His resolve was unwavering, and his commitment was unparalleled.

He tried out again as a junior, and this time he made the varsity team. His efforts had been rewarded, and his journey to basketball greatness had begun. Failure to make the team when he wanted to taught him an important lesson about setbacks and failures as development opportunities.

This early setback taught him the importance of perseverance and practice, a trait he would become known for throughout his career.

Jordan continued his basketball career at the University of North Carolina, where he became a top player. In 1984, he entered the NBA after being selected by the Chicago Bulls in the first round of the NBA Draft. His arrival marked the beginning of an extraordinary journey that would eternally alter the NBA.

When Michael Jordan entered the NBA for the first time, he carried with him a work ethic and dedication to excellence that immediately set him apart. His legendary training approach was instrumental in shaping him into the basketball icon he is today.

Jordan realized that in order to be the greatest, he would have to work harder than anyone else. He had an insatiable desire for growth. During his early NBA career with the Chicago Bulls, he was frequently the first to arrive and the last to exit practice. However, it wasn't enough that he arrived early and stayed late; it also mattered what he did during those hours.

His training regimens were grueling. He would practice his accuracy, dribbling, and defensive skills with unmatched energy. He would take thousands of shots per day in an effort to refine his technique. However, being competent wasn't enough for him; he wanted to be the best.

His teammates and coaches admired his dedication and his commitment to training inspired those around him to pursue excellence. Not only was he a leader on the court, but he also set the standard for what it meant to work hard and never settle for mediocrity in practice.

But the game was about more than just the physical aspect. Jordan was a basketball student, continually analyzing his opponents and the game itself. He had a profound understanding of strategy and utilized his basketball intelligence to outwit his opponents.

The 1998 NBA Finals were one of Michael's most famous games. The Chicago Bulls held a 3-2 series advantage over the Utah Jazz. The Bulls needed a victory in Game 6 to secure the championship.

As if written in the stars, a moment was about to be immortalized during the final few seconds of the game. With the basketball in his palms, Michael Jordan moved with the grace of a conductor conducting an orchestra. The spectators held their breath, and even the athletes on the court appeared to be transfixed in place.

With time running out, Jordan decided to act. He ascended into the air, suspended like a bird in flight, tongue protruding in his trademark style. The ball escaped his digits and sailed gracefully toward the goal. It appeared as though the entire world ceased in anticipation of the outcome.

And then, a swish!

The projectile caused the net to ripple as it passed through. The crowd erupted in a deafening clamor, and Jordan triumphantly raised his fist in the air. The Chicago Bulls had won both the game and the title. The arena was filled with excitement as fans, teammates, and even opponents paid tribute to Michael Jordan's greatness.

It was a transcendent moment in basketball. It was a reminder that with unwavering determination, practice, and a champion's spirit, the impossible can be accomplished. The shot became a symbol of Jordan's unrivaled skill, competitiveness, and clutch performances in the most crucial moments. It was a shot that would be viewed and celebrated for generations, a testament to Michael Jordan's brilliance and the NBA's thrilling drama.

The career of Michael Jordan was filled with instances like this. With the Chicago Bulls, he won six NBA championships, received numerous MVP accolades, and became a global icon. His commitment, perseverance, and unwavering attitude are what made him not only a basketball legend but also a global inspiration. Remember the story of Michael Jordan and how he transformed setbacks into legendary comebacks whenever you face your next challenge.

2

LEBRON JAMES - 2013 NBA FINALS GAME 6

The sixth game of the 2013 NBA Finals was a monumental event, and LeBron James was at the center of it. The Miami Heat and the San Antonio Spurs were engaged in a fiercely fought championship series, and the stakes were high. With mere seconds remaining, the Heat were trailing, and their championship hopes hung in the balance. But suddenly, LeBron had possession of the ball, and the entire basketball world held its breath.

LeBron Raymone James was born in Akron, Ohio, on December 30, 1984. He grew up with a passion for basketball, and it didn't take long for everyone to recognize his talent. However, LeBron had a difficult upbringing. Due to financial instability, his family frequently moved from apartment to apartment. Occasionally, they even stayed with friends or family. LeBron's early years were marked by determination and attentiveness to his game. He was aware that basketball could be his ticket to a better life, and he was willing to put forth the necessary effort. He had no idea that his passion for basketball would propel him to the pinnacle of the sport, where he would become an NBA legend.

Regardless of where he lived, LeBron always held a basketball. From an early age, he cherished the sport and would play basketball at local courts and in youth competitions. People immediately recognized his exceptional talent since he was taller, quicker, and more skilled than the most kids his age.

Gloria James, his mother, was his rock. She raised him as a single parent, however, she constantly encouraged LeBron to do his best and continue working diligently. As a child, he even received his own basketball hoop as a gift, and he would practice for hours.

His talent became even more evident as he got older. He became a basketball prodigy for his high school team, St. Vincent-St. Mary High School. He was powerful, fast on his feet, and an incredible passer. People began to nickname him "King James" because he played basketball like a king.

The entrance of LeBron James into the NBA was nothing short of historic.

LeBron's path to the NBA began in 2003, when he declared himself draft-eligible. Even though he was only 18 years old, his aptitude and potential could not be denied. That year, the Cleveland Cavaliers had the privilege of selecting him first in the lottery, and they knew they had a once-in-a-lifetime opportunity to bring on a powerful player.

On June 26, 2003, LeBron James was selected first overall in the NBA Draft. He was about to make a monumental transition from high school basketball to the professional league. As he donned a Cavaliers headgear and posed for photographs, the entire basketball community watched-- his entry into the NBA was met with high expectations.

LeBron's early days in the league signaled the emergence of a new basketball superstar. Not only did he perform well, but he played like a seasoned pro. In his very first season, he won the NBA Rookie of the Year award, proving to everyone that he was not just another athlete-- but a future legend.

However, throughout his early years in the NBA, LeBron James encountered a number of formidable obstacles. On his young shoulders rested enormous expectations, with the entire world watching to see if he could live up to the high standards set. When he joined the NBA, he was one of the youngest players, which meant he had a great deal to learn in order to compete at that level. LeBron had to deal with intense scrutiny from the media and his opponents, as well as constant criticism. In addition, he had to adjust to the NBA's faster pace, more complex strategies, and more seasoned opponents. However, LeBron's maturity, work ethic, and basketball IQ enabled him to overcome these obstacles and set the groundwork for his future success as a legendary basketball player.

When playing for the Miami Heat in Game 6 of the 2013 NBA Finals, one of LeBron's most exciting moments occurred. As The Heat trailed by 3 points with only seconds remaining, the entire world fixed their eyes on Lebron.

As he dribbled up the court with the game fading away, LeBron was the picture of concentration and determination. As he crossed half-court, he gazed intently at the basket. It appeared as though he had no escape from the Spurs' suffocating defense. However, LeBron was a maestro on the court, and he knew precisely what to do.

With only a few seconds remaining, LeBron made his play. He took a step back, beyond the three-point line, and released the ball. The entire arena appeared to pause its breath as the basketball flew through the air.

And then it occurred – the ball slipped through the net!

The audience immediately erupted in a deafening roar.

LeBron was not finished during the overtime period. He made yet another remarkable shot, ensuring the Heat's victory. It was a performance for the ages, one that would define his career in the NBA.

His game-tying three-pointer and overtime scoring were nothing short of legendary-- a demonstration of his clutch abilities and his ability to shine under duress. Like LeBron, you too will have moments where your skills are called into action, so it's important to always be prepared through continual practice and determination to be at your best.

3

KAREEM ABDUL JABAR - A SCORING RECORD BROKEN

On the evening of April 5, 1984, in Salt Lake City, the stage was set for history to be made when the Los Angeles Lakers played the Utah Jazz. Kareem Abdul-Jabbar was on the brink of entering the record books as one of the greatest basketball players of all time.

Born on April 16, 1947, in New York City, Kareem Abdul-Jabbar was came into the world with the name Ferdinand Lewis Alcindor Jr. Kareem was extraordinarily tall from a young age, and he utilized his height to his full advantage on the basketball court. By the time he was 13, he could already slam dunk a ball being six foot eight inches! He led his high school team to 71 consecutive victories while playing for Power Memorial Academy. Can you imagine such a huge streak of victories? It was evident that Kareem possessed a unique quality. After scoring a total of 2067 total points for the New York City Power Memorial Academy, he earned the nickname "The Tower from Power".

Before Kareem Abdul-Jabbar began his tenure in the NBA, he faced a number of challenging obstacles. At a young age, he lost his father, leaving him with a profound emptiness in his life. In addition, growing up in the racially charged atmosphere of the 1950s and 1960s, Kareem was a witness to racial discrimination and segregation. His extraordinary height, while advantageous for basketball, also made him feel out of place in his younger years. As he pursued his education, he attended a predominantly white Catholic secondary school, Power Memorial Academy, while navigating the challenges of racial integration. His transition from high school to college at UCLA marked a turning point in his life, as he embraced Islam and adopted the name Kareem Abdul-Jabbar.

When he attended UCLA for college, his talents began to flourish. He became the nation's best collegiate athlete after capturing three consecutive NCAA titles. With such achievements, basketball fans were eager to see his future NBA performance.

The Milwaukee Bucks selected Kareem as the first overall selection in the 1969 NBA Draft. His entry into the league was as dramatic as a thunderstorm. As the Rookie of the Year, he was an instant sensation.

His skill was immediately apparent in 1969 as a rookie. Kareem wasn't just towering-- he was also extraordinarily skilled. Many opponents found it virtually impossible to block his skyhook shot, for which he was renowned. Not only did he score, but he was also an excellent defender and shot-blocker.

The early years of Kareem's NBA career were extraordinary, but they were not without challenges. With such an incredible debut, Kareem's expectations were sky-high, and the pressure to perform at an exceptional level was ongoing. He also had to adjust to the league's physical demands and fierce competition in order to compete against such legendary NBA players as Bill Russell and Wilt Chamberlain.

In addition to challenges on the court, Kareem was constantly watched and scrutinized by the media, which can be quite intense. Even though professional success came early in his career, he did not win an NBA championship until joining the Los Angeles Lakers in 1980.

On the historic evening of April 5, 1984, the Los Angeles Lakers and the Utah Jazz faced off in Salt Lake City. The stage was set for history to be made and Kareem Abdul-Jabbar was close to entering the record books. He was attempting to break Wilt Chamberlain's record for the most career points scored in the NBA, and the basketball world was buzzing with excitement. It became evident as the game progressed that this was a momentous occasion.

The dynamic point guard for the Lakers, Magic Johnson, dribbled down the court late in the second quarter. He located Kareem in the post with a swift pass. The 7-foot-2-

inch legend squared off against the 7-foot-4-inch shot-blocking specialist Mark Eaton, who was a formidable opponent.

Kareem, renowned for his elegant and virtually unstoppable skyhook shot, made his move. With remarkable finesse, he rose above the defense and fired his trademark shot from 15 feet out. The crowd held its breath as the basketball ascended through the air, arcing gracefully toward the basket.

It was a SMASH!

The audience erupted in thunderous applause as the ball sailed through the net. Kareem Abdul-Jabbar completed the task. He surpassed Wilt Chamberlain's NBA record for most points scored in a career. It was a moment in history that forever changed the sport.

Kareem's record-breaking basket signified the culmination of a legendary career and the epitome of excellence in the world of basketball.

But Kareem was not only a basketball standout. He was a scholar and author who wrote on a variety of topics. In addition, he was a wonderful ambassador for the sport, demonstrating that basketball could lead to a variety of opportunities to spark social change. Kareem's story is a lesson in how hard work, talent, and a passion for the game can lead you to incredible heights on and off the basketball court.

4

WILT CHAMBERLAIN - THE 100 POINT GAME

O n the frigid evening of March 2, 1962, history was about to be made in the cozy Hershey Sports Arena in Hershey, Pennsylvania. Wilt Chamberlain was playing for the Philadelphia Warriors against the New York Knicks in a game that would write his name in the record books.

Born in Philadelphia, Pennsylvania on August 21, 1936. Wilt was a towering presence in the game. At 7 feet 1 inch tall, he was an absolute giant compared to other players. However, his height was not his only superpower; he was also extremely athletic and talented. People dubbed him "The Big Dipper" due to his unmatched ability to vault the basketball.

Wilt Chamberlain's early life was characterized by many obstacles that would come to shape him as a man and basketball player. Born in Philadelphia in 1936, he grew up during a time of racial discrimination and segregation in the

United States. As an African-American, he was forced to face the harsh realities of a segregated society, experiencing first-hand the indignities and inequalities that people of color experience. These early encounters with prejudice would inspire Chamberlain to advocate for civil rights and social justice further into his career.

However, Chamberlain had to contend with more than just societal difficulties. His physical attributes made him stand out from an early age. Even as a child, he was exceptionally tall, which often made him feel uncomfortable and out of place. Throughout his childhood, he was forced to confront the social difficulties of being the "tallest kid in the room."

In a tragic turn of events, Chamberlain lost his adored sister Barbara in a heartbreaking accident when he was only eight years old. This loss had a profound effect on him and his family, as he had to endure emotional heartbreak.

Chamberlain attended Overbrook High School, a pioneering institution in Philadelphia's desegregated public education system. As he adapted to a distinct social and academic environment, this experience of integration, while progressive at the time, presented its own set of social challenges. Regardless, the early basketball career of Wilt Chamberlain was nothing short of extraordinary. When he was a senior in high school, he was already a basketball superstar. He led his Overbrook High School team in Philadelphia to win two city championships while serving as team captain. His towering stature and extraordinary basketball abilities made him an immediate standout.

His transition from high school to the University of Kansas was yet another turning point. As the school had an increased standard of competition and restructured basketball program, Wilt had to make adjustments. It marked the beginning of his basketball prominence, even though he had to adapt to their style of playing.

During his sophomore season, Wilt led the Jayhawks to the NCAA championship game-- where they came agonizingly close to winning. Despite the defeat, his skill was unmistakable, and it became increasingly apparent that he was destined for basketball greatness.

Ultimately, the NBA couldn't wait to have him, and the Philadelphia Warriors selected him with the first overall selection in the 1959 NBA Draft. His entrance into the division was sensational. He was named NBA Rookie of the Year for his rookie season averages of 37.6 points and 27 rebounds per game. Without question, he was a phenomenon-- his scoring and rebounding abilities were unparalleled in the history of the league.

However, obstacles did arise. Despite his individual success, Chamberlain was unable to lead the Warriors to an NBA championship. In the 1966-67 season, he joined the Philadelphia 76ers, where he finally won that elusive championship.

Wilt Chamberlain was renowned in the NBA for both his scoring ability and his competitive nature with Bill Russell of the Boston Celtics-- stoking a public fierce rivalry between the two titans.

Wilt Chamberlain also confronted racial challenges and discrimination off the basketball court as an African American player during a turbulent period for civil rights in the United States. However, he demonstrated that basketball players can be influential leaders off the court by not being afraid to use his platform to advocate for equality and civil rights.

On March 2, 1962, Wilt Chamberlain accomplished something that no one believed was possible-- destined for something exceptional. Early in the game, Wilt was unstoppable while playing for the Philadelphia Warriors against the New York Knicks.

As fans anxiously anticipated the next move of the Big Dipper, the atmosphere in the arena was electrifying.

Wilt was unmatched from the opening tip off. He was effortlessly leaping, grabbing offensive rebounds, and scoring with amazing accuracy. His incredible combination of stature and agility left the Knicks defenseless.

As the game progressed, Wilt's point total points scored rose steadily. He consistently made shots, dominating in the paint and at the foul line. It was a performance that almost seemed supernatural. Every time a basket was made, the audience erupted in awe.

During that game, Wilt Chamberlain scored 100 points in a single game as the final seconds ticked away-- a feat that no one believed was possible. He had accomplished the inconceivable. He made an incredible 36 of 63 field goals and 28 of 32 free throws.

Wilt's historic performance not only established a new NBA single-game scoring record, but it also cemented his status as a basketball legend. Wilt Chamberlain inscribed his name into the record books after the Philadelphia Warriors defeated the New York Knicks with a final score of 169-147.

The 100-point game remains one of the most remarkable achievements in sports history-- a testament to Wilt Chamberlain's extraordinary talent and dominance as a basketball titan. Wilt wasn't just a scorer; he was also a formidable defender and rebounding powerhouse. He led the league in rebounds and was renowned for his ability to block shots.

Wilt Chamberlain's life exemplifies how perseverance, aptitude, and a passion for the game can propel one to incredible heights. His dominance in the NBA, remarkable scoring ability, and towering presence on the court make him one of the all-time greats-- where his legacy continues to inspire basketball players of all ages.

5

TIM DUNCAN - 2003 NBA FINALS

G ame 6 of the 2003 NBA Finals was a nail-biting matchup that would go down in history as one of Tim Duncan's most memorable moments in his career. The San Antonio Spurs were facing the New Jersey Nets, and they had a chance to win the championship-- but it wouldn't be easy. The game had been intense from the very beginning. As the score remained tied, the game came down to a final, crucial possession. The tension in the arena was palpable, and spectators held their breath, knowing that this moment could determine the outcome of the series.

On the court, Tim Duncan, the stoic commander of the Spurs, was a towering presence. His height was 6 feet 11 inches, however his demeanor was known for being calm and collected. As the clock ticked down to the last minutes, he dribbled the ball up the court, knowing full well that the championship hung on his shoulders. Duncan came to a stop upon crossing the free-throw line. In that instant, he made a decision that would forever engrave his name into basketball lore.

Tim Duncan was born in Christiansted, a small community in the U.S. Virgin Islands, on April 25, 1976. Tim was not your conventional basketball superstar; he was frequently referred to as "The Big Fundamental" due to his solid, no-nonsense playing style. He was tall, measuring 6 feet 11 inches in height, and had a knack for getting the smallest details of the game correct.

Tim Duncan's early years, however, were not free of challenges. Growing up in the U.S. Virgin Islands, he encountered obstacles that influenced his personality and work ethic. The devastation caused by Hurricane Hugo in 1989, which severely damaged his home and forced his family to reside in a shelter, was one of those most significant obstacles. Rebuilding his life, this experience taught Duncan resilience and the value of hard work.

In addition, Duncan was considered a late bloomer when he began playing basketball in high school. He didn't begin playing until he was an adolescent-- where his initial focus was on swimming, another sport in which he excelled. In order to keep up with players who had been on the court for years, more focused effort was required of him to transition to basketball.

Despite these obstacles, Duncan's talent and perseverance stood out. At Wake Forest University, he confronted the challenge of competing against some of the nation's most competitive college basketball players. However, Duncan rose to the challenge-- on the court, he was a dominant force due to his dedication and unwavering commitment to developing his game.

Tim Duncan's time at Wake Forest University was a turning point in his professional basketball career. When he arrived at the college, he was a relative novice in basketball, having begun playing in his mid-teens. Despite his late entry into the university's basketball program-- where he soon made a name for himself and left a permanent mark.

Duncan was known for his "Big Fundamental" playing approach, which emphasized the fundamentals needed to win games and doing maneuvers correctly-- a strategy that quickly distinguished him from others. He became a dominant force on the court-- especially on defense, where he excelled at blocking shots and grabbing rebounds.

Duncan was a two-time ACC (Atlantic Coast Conference) Player of the Year and a consensus First-Team All-American during his collegiate career. In 1997, he also claimed the Naismith College Player of the Year award, solidifying his position as one of the nation's top college basketball players.

Despite Duncan's individual success, his Wake Forest team never won an NCAA title, but his influence was monumental. His time at the university set the stage for his future achievement and prepared him for a successful NBA career. Tim Duncan's career at Wake Forest exemplifies the effectiveness of hard work, dedication, and a commitment to the game's fundamentals.

As the first overall pick in the 1997 NBA draft, Tim Duncan confronted high expectations in his early days with the San Antonio Spurs. However, he lived up to the hype, winning NBA Rookie of the Year and rapidly becoming a team leader.

Tim Duncan's legacy as one of the finest basketball players of all time was cemented during Game 6 of the 2003 NBA Finals. The San Antonio Spurs were ahead in their series with the New Jersey Nets, 3-2. One more victory would crown them NBA champions.

Both teams fought for every point in a tense game. As the clock wound down, it became evident that the outcome of this game would come down to the last remaining seconds. The Spurs had possession of the ball with the score deadlocked and the championship on the line.

Tim Duncan, "The Big Fundamental," was the source of hope during this tense moment. With his 6-foot-11 frame, he dribbled the ball with determination up the court. The stakes were high, and everyone in the arena held their breath.

As he neared the free-throw line, Duncan took action. He stopped, rose for a jump shot, and fired the ball with flawless form. As the basketball flew through the air, it was as if time had stopped. And then-- it struck the cage and dropped through the net. When the buzzer sounded, the audience erupted in a deafening roar.

Not only had the Spurs won the game, but they had also clinched the NBA title. The decisive moment was Tim Duncan's clutch shot, and he was named Finals MVP for his remarkable performance throughout the series. The Spurs' triumph was a result of his "Big Fundamental" style and court leadership.

Tim Duncan's uniqueness was not limited to his basketball skills-- his humility, dedication to his team, and unwavering work ethic were well-known within the NBA. He spent his entire career with the Spurs, demonstrating that greatness can be achieved while remaining devoted to oneself.

Game 6 of the 2003 NBA Finals shows how the determination and talent of a single basketball player can make all the difference. The legacy of Tim Duncan continues to motivate young players to work diligently, be humble, and strive for greatness. His story is a lesson in hard work, doing the fundamentals correctly, and teamwork -- a legacy that continues to be an inspiration for future players today.

6

HAKEEM OLAJUWON - 1994 WESTERN CONFERENCE FINALS

Hakeem Olajuwon, also known as "The Dream," played a critical role in Game 7 of the 1994 Western Conference Finals, which will forever be remembered in NBA history. The Houston Rockets were caught in a winner-take-all matchup with the surging Phoenix Suns.

It was immediately apparent that Hakeem had arrived to perform. His movements were a work of art, a mesmerizing blend of brute force and dexterity. He maneuvered past defenders with a grace that shadowed his towering stature, and he ascended for offensive rebounds with the heart of a man driven to score. The Suns responded and hurled everything they had at Hakeem-- but he appeared invulnerable.

Hakeem was born on January 21, 1963 in Lagos, Nigeria. His story is as motivational as they come.

Hakeem was dubbed "The Dream," and his journey in basketball was certainly that-- a dream come true. He had a distinctive technique that combined strength and grace, and he was able to accomplish feats on the court that no one else could.

Early in life, Hakeem encountered financial difficulties. He did not come from a privileged background and confronted situations where he lacked sufficient funds for basic needs. This upbringing instilled in him a strong work ethic and a profound appreciation for the worth of success earned through hard work.

Hakeem played for the University of Houston and helped lead the Cougars to the 1983 NCAA championship game after relocating to the United States for college. Even though they lost, his extraordinary talent was impossible to overlook.

The journey of Hakeem Olajuwon from Lagos, Nigeria to NBA stardom was filled with obstacles, each of which contributed to the creation of a basketball legend. Hakeem did not start playing basketball until he was a teenager, which was a late start compared to his rivals. While other future NBA players were honing their talents at a young age, Hakeem was still focusing on Nigerian soccer. This meant he had to work twice as hard to catch up and master the game he would eventually dominate.

Hakeem moved to the United States in his late teens to pursue a collegiate education and a basketball career. Nonetheless, this presented a brand-new set of obstacles--language was one of the first challenges he encountered. Since English was not his native tongue, and he had to get used to a new culture as well as a new language. He ultimately had to adapt to a new way of life, including customs, food, and social conventions.

When he enrolled at the University of Houston to play college basketball, he confronted the challenge of adjusting to the fast-paced and intensely competitive American college basketball scene. This was a brand-new world for him-- one that required unrelenting effort and a sharp learning curve.

Despite these obstacles, Hakeem's tenacity, work ethic, and natural basketball ability set him on the path to prominence. These early adversities were the fire in which his character was forged, making him a living example of how the capacity to overcome obstacles can lead to extraordinary accomplishments.

In 1984, he was selected first overall by the Houston Rockets in the NBA Draft. This is when his NBA career began. His incredible abilities led him through an amazing career where he was also renowned for his generosity and sportsmanship—as well as his extraordinary agility on the court.

Ten years later, Game 7 of the 1994 Western Conference Finals was the moment that cemented his legacy. The stakes could not have been higher for the matchup between the Houston Rockets and the formidable Phoenix Suns. This game would determine which teams would advance to the NBA finals.

Hakeem's goal was evident from the moment he received the tip. His footwork was extraordinary, a mesmerizing display of agility and strength. He dribbled past defenders, soared for offensive rebounds, and executed flawless moves that left both spectators and opponents amazed.

The high-scoring offense of the Suns hurled everything they had at Olajuwon, but he was unstoppable. He blocked shots with his signature shot-blocking prowess and scored with grace and dexterity.

As the game neared the final seconds, the score was tied. The arena was filled with tension, and the world watched. With only a few seconds remaining on the clock and the Rockets trailing by two points, Hakeem gained possession of the ball.

He demonstrated the abilities of a guard in the body of a center by dribbling with poise. Then, just before the siren, he executed a picture-perfect jump shot that left the Suns' defenders bewildered. As the projectile arced through the air, time appeared to stop. It sailed through the rim with nothing but net, clinching the game for the Rockets and propelling them to victory.

The audience erupted in a frenzy of applause, and the Rockets qualified for the NBA Finals.

Hakeem Olajuwon was dubbed the NBA Finals Most Valuable Player for his outstanding performance in that series and for leading the Rockets to their first-ever NBA title. In his winning Game 7 performance, his fast moves, coordinated footwork, and unmatched flow around the defense secured his place among basketball legends.

His journey from Lagos, Nigeria, to NBA stardom serves as an inspiration to young athletes around the globe, demonstrating that dreams can come true with hard work, dedication, and a little basketball magic. His legacy continues to inspire future generations of basketball athletes.

7

LARRY BIRD - 1986 NBA FINALS

G ame 6 of the 1986 NBA Finals was a night to remember, and at the center of it all was Larry Bird-- the Boston Celtics' beating heart. The championship was incredibly close as the Boston Celtics faced the Houston Rockets.

From the very start, Bird had a mission. And it was seen in his performance during this game. His accuracy was nothing short of extraordinary, and he had an almost supernatural touch with the basketball. He buried three-pointers with the aim of a marksman. His passes were a work of art-- setting up easy baskets for his teammates.

Born on 7 December 1956, in West Baden Springs, Indiana, Larry Bird was a legend in the making. His story is one of hard work, devotion, and a deep passion for the game.

Beginning in the small Indiana town of French Lick, Larry Bird's early days are a tale of triumph over adversity. Living in a modest home with limited resources, the Bird family struggled financially. This frugal upbringing instilled in Larry an unwavering work ethic and a profound appreciation for the value of perseverance.

The small-town atmosphere of French Lick also posed an additional obstacle. It lacked the thriving basketball culture of larger communities, so Bird did not have access to the same level of competition or coaching as other players. Therefore, he had to compensate for the lack of opportunities through sheer determination-- practicing tirelessly by himself and with friends.

Frequently undervalued, Bird's overlooked talent added to the struggle. Despite his extraordinary abilities, he initially slipped under the radar of major college programs, primarily due to his small-town upbringing and limited exposure.

College scouts and coaches, who frequently evaluate talent in more prominent areas, did not consider him to be a top prospect. This meant Larry Bird had to continuously prove himself on the court through his skills, work ethic, and dedication to the game. Despite these early challenges, Bird's resolve and passion for the game remained steadfast. Not to mention, his skills were too exceptional to remain concealed for long.

In 1975, he enrolled at Indiana State University, where the Sycamores quickly realized they were dealing with a once-in-a-lifetime talent. The effect of Bird was immediate. In his junior year, he was named team captain, and under his direction, the Sycamores attained remarkable success. Bird was the Missouri Valley Conference Player of the Year three times and a unanimous First Team All-American.

Bird's college career reached its peak in 1979, when he led Indiana State to the NCAA championship game. The game between the Sycamores and Michigan State, spearheaded by Magic Johnson, was dubbed "Magic vs. Bird." It was one of the most-watched college basketball games in history, and it helped propel both players to NBA stardom. Even though Indiana State did not win the championship, Bird's performance was extraordinary.

The college statistics of Bird were astounding. He averaged over 30 points per game and collected over 13 rebounds. On the court, his scoring prowess, basketball IQ, and versatility were unmatched. Bird had a significant impact—he demonstrated that players from smaller schools could compete and become superstars at the highest level.

Despite the difficulties he encountered in his early years as a result of his small-town upbringing, Bird's unyielding work ethic and commitment to the sport paved the way for an illustrious NBA career.

The Boston Celtics selected him sixth overall in the 1978 draft. Bird's effect on the NBA was immediate-- his extraordinary shooting, passing, and basketball IQ were unmatched. During his rookie year, he transformed the

Celtics from a struggling team to a true championship contender.

The sixth game of the 1986 NBA Finals would go down in history as one of Larry Bird's most iconic performances. The Boston Celtics were competing against the Houston Rockets, and the NBA championship was within reach. Larry Bird, the Celtics' heart and spirit, was determined to make this a night to remember.

Bird was on fire from the initial tip-off. His shooting was nothing short of an act of sorcery. He had an uncanny ability to make three-pointers from anywhere on the court. Just as mesmerizing, his passes enabled his colleagues to score with relative ease. Ultimately, it was his leadership and determination that truly distinguished him.

The tension in the Boston Garden was tense as the game came down to the wire. The Celtics held a minor advantage, and the spectators were on the edge of their seats. Larry Bird made a play that will go down in basketball lore with seconds remaining on the clock.

With the Rockets frantically attempting to score, Bird anticipated a pass, made a clutch interception, and then, in a single fluid motion, he delivered a perfect pass to Dennis Johnson-- who dashed down the court and made a breakaway layup at the final buzzer.

A deafening roar erupted from the arena. The game was won by the Celtics, and Larry Bird's steal and assist sealed their championship victory! That night's performance by Bird was nothing short of legendary-- he completed the game with 29 points, 11 rebounds, and 12 assists. It was a triple-double that showcased his extraordinary all-around skills.

Larry Bird's impact on the game was far greater than his impressive statistics indicate. He was renowned for his work ethic, basketball intelligence, and capacity to improve his teammates. His unwavering competitiveness and leadership were the embodiment of what it meant to be a Boston Celtic.

Game 6 of the 1986 NBA Finals was more than a victory; it was a demonstration of Larry Bird's unbreakable spirit and skill. It continues to serve as a source of motivation for young basketball players, demonstrating that greatness on the court can be accomplished with hard work, a never-quit mentality, and a passion for the game.

Larry Bird's life is a resounding example of how even the most difficult early circumstances can be overcome with unwavering dedication to one's dreams.

8

SHAQUILLE O'NEAL - 2000 NBA FINALS

I n a warm June of 2000, the Los Angeles Lakers and Indiana Pacers engaged in an enthralling NBA Finals matchup. Shaquille O'Neal, the towering force of the Lakers, was at the core of this epic showdown. Shaq, as his fans affectionately nicknamed him, was prepared to leave his mark on the championship series. Both teams gave their all, making the game a nail-biter. In the decisive final minutes of the game, the Lakers held a razor-thin lead. The Staples Center buzzed with anticipation. This could be the decisive moment in their NBA championship victory.

Born on March 6th 1972, in Newark, New Jersey, Shaq was destined for greatness. Growing to 7 feet 1 inch tall, by the time he was an adolescent, he was already taller than the majority of adults.

Shaquille O'Neal's early years were marked by a combination of financial struggles, extraordinary physical stature, and academic difficulties-- all of which he overcame on his remarkable journey to basketball superstardom.

Shaq's upbringing was frequently blemished by financial struggles. There were instances when his family had to make do with very little because of their situation. These early experiences instilled in Shaq a strong work ethic and resilience-- as he came to appreciate the value of hard work and the significance of perseverance in the face of adversity.

Even as a young child, Shaquille's towering stature made him stand out. However, his height was a double-edged sword. Being extraordinarily tall made it difficult for him to blend in with children his age and find his place in social settings. On the basketball court, however, it was precisely this physical trait that would prove to be his greatest asset.

Early on, Shaq was also confronted with academic difficulties. He struggled academically, and balancing his blooming basketball career with his academics required a great deal of effort and commitment. This required extensive time spent practicing both on the court and in the classroom.

Shaquille O'Neal's college years were marked by both triumphs and tribulations, ultimately establishing the groundwork for his incredible success in basketball. Shaq, a standout high school athlete, had his choice of college teams, but ultimately chose to play for the LSU Tigers at the Louisiana State University.

His college achievements were nothing short of extraordinary. In his sophomore year, he was already displaying the potential to become a basketball legend. Shaq was recognized as the College Player of the Year, a distinction that reflected his dominance on the court. He was an intimidating force in college basketball due to his stature, strength, and abilities. Fans and NBA scouts were equally impressed with his play.

Shaq's undergraduate years were not, however, without difficulties. Both the academic rigors of college and the pressures of being a basketball sensation presented obstacles for him. It took incredible effort and commitment for him to balance the rigors of his studies with those of his all consuming athletic career. Shaq met the challenge head-on, and it would teach him valuable lessons about time management and perseverance.

Despite these obstacles, Shaquille O'Neal's undergraduate years prepared him for his future career. His outstanding performances on the court and ability to rise to the occasion when it mattered the most made him an adored figure in LSU basketball history. His time at LSU would pave the way for his entrance into the NBA, where he would go on to become one of the most dominant players in the league.

Shaquille O'Neal's early days in the NBA were characterized by a combination of high expectations and difficult obstacles. Shaq, who was selected by the Orlando Magic with the first overall selection in the 1992 NBA Draft, bore a heavy burden of high expectations. From the beginning, he was under a tremendous amount of pressure to perform at an elite level and lead his team to greatness.

Shaq was no exception to the fact that the transition from college to the professional levels is difficult for all athletes. He had to adjust to the NBA season's accelerated speed, increased competition, and demanding schedule. Shaq was moving into uncharted territory in the NBA.

Shaq's free-throw marksmanship was one of his most notorious early career struggles. They frequently employed a strategy known as "Hack-a-Shaq," intentionally striking him because they knew he struggled with free throws. This strategy became a significant source of conflict and frustration for Shaq and his teammates.

However, despite these early obstacles, Shaq's extraordinary talent and unyielding perseverance were readily apparent. On the court, he was a force to be reckoned with due to his size and distinct combination of power and flair. He established himself as one of the league's most dominant centers by consistently averaging double-doubles. Even though his early NBA career was marked by both victories and setbacks, they played a crucial role in molding him into the dominant and resilient player he later became.

The year 2000 marked the beginning of one of the most epic NBA Finals matchups. Shaquille O'Neal, the Los Angeles Lakers' colossus, was about to face the Indiana Pacers. The pressure was readily apparent as the Lakers were about to secure an NBA championship.

As the series finale progressed, it became evident that this would be a battle for the ages. The Lakers held a razor-thin lead, and the Staples Center was nearly suffocating with tension-- every pass, shot, and rebound felt like a potential game-changer.

Shaq found himself engulfed by defenders beneath the basket with mere seconds remaining. The pressure intensified. Then, like a bolt of lightning from the sky, he soared above the opposition and slammed the ball through the rim with tremendous force. The dunk rocked the arena to its foundations and electrified the crowd.

It was a moment that would live on forever.

This dunk added two more points to Shaq's already remarkable nightly total. The fact that he completed the game with 41 points demonstrates that he was the dominant force on the court. Shaq was dubbed Finals MVP, not only for that game but for his incredible performance throughout the entire series-- as the Lakers won the championship.

Shaq's performance in the 2000 NBA Finals was not only a testament to his immense stature-- but also to his ability to perform under pressure. His agility, strength, and scoring prowess rendered him unstoppable. Shaq's legacy as one of the most dominant players in NBA history was solidified by his iconic dunk in the final seconds of the game.

Shaquille O'Neal's rise from a towering adolescent to an NBA superstar is a tale of perseverance, hard work, and utilizing one's unique talents to achieve distinction. He demonstrated that it is more important to have a big heart and a sense of humor to match one's size. Shaq leaves an unmistakable impression on and off the basketball court and continues to inspire young players.

9

DIRK NOWITZKI - 2011 NBA FINALS GAME 5

In the pivotal Game 5 of the 2011 NBA Finals, Dirk Nowitzki displayed his basketball abilities in a way that will be immortalized in NBA history. The Dallas Mavericks and the Miami Heat were tied, with the series standing at 2-2.

As the crucial final moments of the game approached, the Mavericks trailed by a single point.

Taking the lead, Dirk delivered an unforgettable performance-- driving his team towards victory with grace and precision.

Dirk Nowitzki was born in Würzburg, Germany, on June 19, 1978. He was extraordinarily tall for his age and was a basketball fanatic as a kid. His height was a distinct advantage, but it also presented a number of obstacles.

On occasion, he struggled to fit in because he towered over his peers, but he quickly realized that his height could be a powerful asset on the basketball court.

Dirk's early days in the sport were anything but simple. He faced skepticism and doubts about his ability to compete at the highest level, primarily due to the fact that he was from Germany, a nation not known for its basketball greatness. Nonetheless, Dirk's unwavering determination and love for the game drove him to disprove the critics.

Before entering the NBA, Dirk did not play college basketball in the United States. Being a German basketball player, he launched his professional career with the DJK Wurzburg in Germany's premiere league-- the Basketball Bundesliga (BBL). During this time, Dirk's decision to forego college and spend a season in the BBL was quite uncommon.

During a promotional game called the Nike Hoop Heroes tour, Dirk played against NBA greats Charles Barkley and Scottie Pippen. In the matchup, Dirk dunked on Barkley, who was impressed by his performance signaling recognition by the NBA. At the time, Dirk was still a teenager-- imagine outplaying a professional like Barkley! Other NBA players were quick to notice his speed, ball handling and shooting range.

When he decided to pursue his dreams of being in the NBA, he faced the challenges of adjusting to a new country and culture. It was difficult for him to leave his home and family behind, and he had to overcome language barriers and cultural adjustments that come with residing in the United States.

Despite these obstacles, Dirk possessed undeniable talent. He honed his abilities, perfected his game, and worked relentlessly to accomplish his objectives. His early years of adversity only strengthened his will, leading him to become one of the greatest power forwards in NBA history.

As Dirk grew older, his court talents attracted the attention of basketball scouts. In 1998, he joined the Dallas Mavericks of the NBA, and the rest is history.

Early in his NBA career, Dirk Nowitzki faced the challenges of adapting to a new league and showcasing his unique abilities. He was a relatively unknown German athlete when he was drafted by the Milwaukee Bucks with the ninth overall pick in the 1998 NBA Draft and then traded to the Dallas Mavericks on the same day. Many questioned whether a European player, particularly one of his stature at 7 feet tall, could succeed in the physically demanding and fiercely competitive NBA.

Nevertheless, Dirk's arrival in Dallas signified the beginning of something extraordinary. He immediately demonstrated the talent and work ethic necessary to succeed in the NBA. His outside shooting, court agility, and versatility with plays were a remarkable, and he quickly became one of the most dominant players in the league. Dirk's sheer determination to his craft propelled him to success, despite the difficulties that many NBA rookies encounter-- like adjusting to the league's faster pace.

Game 5 of the 2011 NBA Finals was pivotal for Dirk Nowitzki and the Dallas Mavericks. The series was tied 2-2 against the impressive Miami Heat, and Game 5 was expected to be decisive.

That night, Dirk was nothing short of phenomenal. He appeared on fire, making shot after shot-- as the Mavericks needed every point he could produce. As the final seconds trickled away, the Mavericks trailed by one point with the game on the line.

Then came the decisive moment.

With the ball in his possession, Dirk inhaled deeply and made his move. With his eyes fixed on the basket, he drove toward it while firmly dribbling the ball. The defenders were unable to stop him, and he placed the ball into the net with graceful dexterity.

As the Mavericks seized the lead, the arena erupted with excitement. Not only did Dirk's layup secure a thrilling victory for his team, but it also cemented his reputation as a clutch performer. He finished the game with an impressive 29 points, demonstrating his ability to perform under pressure.

However, the story doesn't end there. In that season, the Mavericks went on to claim the NBA championship-- and Dirk Nowitzki was named the NBA Finals Most Valuable

Player. His performance in Game 5 was pivotal to that team's championship run, and it remains one of the NBA's most memorable moments.

Dirk Nowitzki's extraordinary abilities, tenacity, and composure in high-pressure situations made him not only an NBA legend, but also a true inspiration to young aspiring basketball players around the globe.

10

KOBE BRYANT - THE 81 POINT GAME

Nobody could have predicted the extraordinary spectacle that was about to transpire between the Los Angeles Lakers and Toronto Raptors on the evening of January 22, 2006. NBA player Kobe Bryant, also known as the "Black Mamba," was about to make history and become a certified legend.

Born in Philadelphia, Pennsylvania on August 23, 1978, basketball was ingrained in Kobe Bryant's DNA from birth. Joe "Jellybean" Bryant, his father, was a former NBA player. Therefore, it was not surprising that Kobe fell in love with basketball and chose to follow in his father's footsteps.

Kobe demonstrated from a young age that he was destined for greatness. He soaked up all the basketball knowledge he could like a sponge. He ignited his basketball career at Lower Merion High School, where he became a local phenomenon.

In 1996, Kobe took a significant risk by entering the NBA directly from high school. He was drafted by the Charlotte Hornets, but was then traded to the Los Angeles Lakers. He would spend his entire 20-year career there, achieving superstar status.

In the early days of Kobe Bryant's illustrious basketball career, he was confronted with a series of formidable obstacles that tested his strength and resiliency. His decision to enter the NBA right out of high school was one of the most challenging obstacles. Kobe was just 17 years old when he was drafted by the Charlotte Hornets and then transferred to the Los Angeles Lakers in 1996. Being so young, many skeptics doubted his ability to compete at the professional level. However, Kobe's unwavering self-confidence and work ethic enabled him to not only flourish but also become one of the sport's greatest stars.

Kobe faced additional difficulty in gaining the faith and respect of his more seasoned teammates. As a young player, he had to demonstrate his commitment and dedication both on and off the court. It was also a learning curve for him to find a balance between his exceptional individual abilities and playing cooperatively with this teammates. Kobe's scoring prowess was recognized, but he had to learn when to share the ball and when to assume control of a game.

As a young player, continuous criticism and comparisons weighed heavily on Kobe's shoulders. Being a high draft decision and rising star, he was subjected to never-ending scrutiny and frequent comparisons to legendary basketball players such as Michael Jordan. These comparisons equally drew both enormous expectations and pressure.

However, it was through these early trials and challenges that Kobe honed his abilities and developed the tenacity that would come to define his career. His talent, coupled with a tireless work ethic and unwavering confidence in his abilities, enabled him to not only overcome these obstacles, but also ascend to greatness. Kobe's journey illustrates the transformative power of commitment, and unwavering self-assurance in overcoming challenges.

Kobe Bryant etched his name into basketball history on January 22, 2006, with a performance that will be remembered for generations. The night started off as a regular-season game between the Los Angeles Lakers and Toronto Raptors, but what transpired was something extraordinary.

Kobe's mission was clear from the opening tip off-- It was as if he had a mysterious connection with the basketball and the remarkable ability to control it. He appeared to defy the principles of gravity with each dribble, jump shot, and dunk.

The Raptors unleashed their entire arsenal against him, but it made no difference. Kobe was in his element. He was a maestro conducting a basket symphony, and the Staples Center was his audience.

As the game progressed, Kobe's point total increased. He had an extraordinary combination of outside shots, brilliant drives to the basket, and ice-cold free throws. The audience collectively held its breath as the moment of truth approached.

Upon hearing the final buzzer, Kobe had accomplished the extraordinary. He tallied 81 points-- the second-highest total in NBA history. It was a performance that left everyone in the arena in astonishment. The Lakers won the game, but Kobe was the genuine victor.

His 81-point performance was symbolic of the power of believing in oneself and possessing the ability to back it up. Kobe demonstrated that with unwavering determination and a passion for the game, one can accomplish the extraordinary. His legacy continues to inspire young athletes to pursue their ambitions and attempt the impossible.

Kobe ultimately achieved five NBA championships and two NBA Finals MVP awards with the Los Angeles Lakers. He was also named to 18 NBA All-Star Teams and 15 All-NBA Teams. Kobe's offensive prowess was legendary-- and for two seasons he led the NBA in scoring.

During the 2015-2016 season, his farewell tour was a tribute to his remarkable career-- concluding it with an unforget-table performance against the Utah Jazz, tallying 60 points. The Los Angeles Staples Center crowd erupted in cheers in honor of one of the game's greatest legends. Kobe's speech at the end of the game--in which he said goodbye to the fans and the sport he so cherished-- was an emotional moment that touched the lives of millions.

In January 2020, just a few years after his retirement, Kobe, his daughter Gianna, and seven others tragically perished in a helicopter accident. The world mourned the passing of a cherished basketball legend. Kobe's legacy continues to live on in the hearts of fans, players, and aspiring athletes worldwide.

11

KARL MALONE - 1998 FINALS GAME 5

June 12, 1998 marked a moment of basketball greatness in the 1998 NBA Finals. At the center of it all was Karl Malone, nicknamed "The Mailman." During this game, the Utah Jazz faced the formidable Chicago Bulls, and the series was tied at 2-2. Game 5 was the decisive turning point, and Karl Malone capitalized on his chance to shine.

Karl Malone was born in Summerfield, Louisiana on July 24, 1963.

Growing up on a farm, he quickly developed a passion for basketball despite his impoverished beginnings. He played collegiate basketball at Louisiana Tech before being drafted in 1985 by the Utah Jazz. Everyone was unaware that he would become one of the game's most dominant performers ever.

However, Karl Malone's journey to NBA greatness truly began in a small Louisiana town. His early years were marked by the difficulties of growing up in a modest, blue collar family. However, his parents imparted in him the values of discipline, responsibility, and the significance of hard work, which would serve as the basis of his future success.

Karl Malone encountered an early obstacle due to the absence of organized basketball in his hometown. To make matters worse, there were no training centers or basketball courts nearby. He had to practice on an improvised hoop affixed to the side of a barn! It was here, often in the sweltering Louisiana humidity, that he practiced dribbling, shooting, and dreaming of a future in basketball.

Karl Malone faced a new obstacle as he grew taller and more skilled-- attracting the attention of college recruiters. Unlike many of his contemporaries, he was not in the national spotlight while playing at Louisiana Tech University. However, his perseverance and tireless work ethic made him stand out. In 1985, he was chosen by the Utah Jazz in the NBA Draft, launching his professional career.

The transition from a small-town farm to the bright lights and intense competition of the NBA marked Malone's early days. Like many rookies, he had to adjust to the NBA's faster tempo and greater physical demands.

As soon as he joined the Utah Jazz in 1985, he established himself as a feared opponent. Malone stood out due to his physicality, unwavering work ethic, and relentless determination. On the court, he was a dominant figure, renowned for his forceful dunks, rebounding prowess, and versatility in scoring. Despite entering the league as a relative unknown, he quickly became one of the most feared and esteemed NBA players.

Malone's partnership with point guard John Stockton became one of the most legendary duos during this era in the NBA. The Utah Jazz's chemistry and cooperation made them a formidable team. Malone's tenacious play on the court, coupled with his consistency and tenacity, made him a forceful All-Star-- allowing him to led the Jazz to multiple postseason appearances and established himself as a scoring juggernaut.

One of Karl's most compelling games occurred on June 12, 1998, when the Jazz played in the NBA Finals against the Chicago Bulls. The championship series was tied at 2-2 in Game 5, creating a pivotal stage in the series.

That night, Karl Malone became an unstoppable force. On the court, he was a juggernaut, scoring from every possible angle and distance. He scored with dunks, jump shots, and layups. However, what made this game truly remarkable was the fact that he played alongside John Stockton. With this duo, the Jazz's offense was in perfect harmony, and Stockton was dishing out assists like a master chef.

Fiercely fought, the game was a back-and-forth struggle in which neither team gave an inch. Every point was valuable, and every possession a turning point. As the game's closing seconds approached, the score was tied. Every spectator in the arena was holding their breath due to the rising tension.

And then, the decisive moment arrived. Karl Malone received a key pass, and with the outcome of the game in doubt, he drove to the basket. It was a high-stakes, heart-pounding aerial launch. The ball blasted from his grasp, sailed through the hoop, and gave the Jazz the lead. The crowd erupted when Karl's heroic play placed the Jazz in front.

However, the battle was not yet over. The Bulls had one last opportunity to steal a victory. However, the Jazz's defense held steadfast, preventing a game-winning attempt by the Bulls. The final buzzer sounded, and with a final tally of 83-81, the Jazz emerged the winners.

Karl Malone's performance was one for the history books. He completed the game with an astounding 39 points, and his clutch performance gave the Jazz the series advantage. Despite the fact that the Bulls ultimately won the championship, Game 5 of the 1998 NBA Finals will eternally be remembered as a testament to Karl Malone's extraordinary skill, determination, and leadership.

Young basketball players continue to be inspired by Karl Malone's legacy as one of the game's all-time greats. He demonstrated that with dedication, passion, and a commitment to excellence, it is possible to achieve greatness on the court.

BILL RUSSELL - 1962 NBA FINALS GAME 7

The year was 1962 and all eyes were fixed on Game 7 of the NBA Finals. In a game that would go down in basketball lore, the Boston Celtics, lead by their legendary captain Bill Russell, were competing against the Los Angeles Lakers.

Bill Russell, a towering presence, was a defensive powerhouse known for his shot-blocking and rebounding skills. But Game 7 wasn't just about his defensive maneuvers; it was an exceptional display of his overall brilliance. Bill was determined to capture the championship when it dangled in the balance.

One of the NBA's all-time finest players, the story of Bill Russell is not only about basketball, but also about leadership, collaboration, and the pursuit of excellence. Born on 12 February 1934 in Monroe, Louisiana, Bill Russell's passion for basketball first took root in California, where he was raised.

Russell faced scholastic difficulties in high school, which jeopardized his athletic eligibility. Meeting the academic requirements to remain eligible was a crucial obstacle he had to surmount, highlighting the significance of balancing sports and education.

In addition, despite his individual ability, Russell was disappointed that he was unable to win a state championship in high school. This setback inspired him to work more diligently to attain team success in college and beyond.

In 1956, the Boston Celtics drafted him after he played collegiate basketball at the University of San Francisco.

In the early days of Bill Russell's basketball career, he faced a number of obstacles that tested his resolve and perseverance. His era's pervasive ethnic discrimination was one of the greatest obstacles he, along with other players, faced. Russell confronted prejudice both on and off the court as an African-American athlete in the 1950s and 1960s. The prejudice he encountered while traveling with his team was emotionally taxing, but it also motivated him to advocate for civil rights and social change.

In addition, Russell's transition to basketball arrived later than that of most players. Prior to his senior year of high school, he was more interested in track and field than basketball. Due to this late start, he had to put forth additional effort to catch up to players who had been honing their skills for a longer time.

Early in his NBA career, Bill Russell was nothing short of spectacular. In 1956, he was drafted by the Boston Celtics, and as soon as he stepped onto NBA court, he made an instantaneous impact. It didn't take him long to become one of the most dominant forces in the league, as his presence on the court was a game-changer.

Russell was an unstoppable defensive force. His shot-blocking and offensive rebounding skills were unparalleled. Even against taller opponents, he was able to brush away shots with remarkable timing and leap to extraordinary heights to secure rebounds. His defensive prowess was the linchpin of a formidable Celtics squad.

Russell's early career in the NBA was characterized by his capacity to perform under pressure. He had a remarkable aptitude for making the decisive plays when it mattered. He was a player who thrived under duress, and his performances in pivotal moments of playoff games are legendary.

One of Bill Russell's most captivating games created a definable moment in basketball history as the Celtics faced off against the Los Angeles Lakers in Game 7 of the 1962 NBA Finals. The series was deadlocked at 3-3-- and this game meant everything.

Bill Russell appeared as a giant throughout the entire series. He consistently secured possession for his team by leaping above the rim to grab offensive rebounds. He was relentless, deflecting shots and imposing his will on the Lakers' offense. His scoring, however, was what made his performance truly legendary.

When it mattered most, Bill Russell, transformed into an offensive force. He scored 30 points, demonstrating a variety of post moves with a relentless determination to land the ball in the basket.

However, it was his rebounding that astonished everyone during the game. Bill Russell grabbed a staggering 40 rebounds, establishing a record that still stands as the most rebounds in an NBA Finals game. Each offensive rebound was evidence of his ability to dominate the boards.

In the game's final seconds, with the score locked, the Celtics looked to their leader. Bill Russell rose to the occasion with a clutch basket that placed the Celtics in the lead. The Lakers had one final opportunity to force overtime, but they were unable to break through Bill's tenacious defense. The final horn rang, and the Celtics were declared champions!

Bill Russell's epic performance in Game 7 of the 1962 NBA Finals was a shining example of leadership, determination, and the ability to deliver when the stakes were at their highest. His 30 points and 40 rebounds in a championship-deciding game continue to represent NBA excellence.

Bill Russell's legacy extends far beyond championships and statistics. He was also a leader who inspired his colleagues and made all those around him perform better. He led the Celtics to 11 NBA titles in 13 years-- a record that holds to this day. Bill's legacy exemplifies the value of teamwork, perseverance, and the ability to rise to the occasion during crucial moments.

13

MAGIC JOHNSON - 1980 NBA FINALS GAME 6

I n Game 6 of the 1980 NBA Finals, the stage was set for an epic battle on the court. The series between the Los Angeles Lakers and the Philadelphia 76ers was tied in a dead heat at 3-3. To make things more intense, the Lakers' superstar, Kareem Abdul-Jabbar, was injured and unable to play. To head the charge, all eyes were on a rookie named Earvin "Magic" Johnson.

Earvin "Magic" Johnson is one of the most riveting NBA athletes of all time. The story of Magic resembles a real-life basketball fairy tale. Magic was born in Lansing, Michigan, on August 14, 1959. At a young age, he had a basketball in his palms and was already displaying the incredible talent for which he would become famous.

Early in his life, Magic Johnson encountered some unique obstacles, but his determination and passion for the game helped him overcome them. In Lansing, Michigan, he grew up in a neighborhood with limited opportunities. Poverty and gang violence were a part of his environment, making it imperative that he maintain his focus on his goals. Moreover, as a young African-American in the 1960s and 1970s, he encountered discrimination and prejudice that served as a reminder of the difficulties he would face. Nonetheless, Magic's love for basketball and commitment to his craft led him to become one of the NBA's most iconic figures. His rise from a difficult upbringing to NBA superstardom is evidence of his determination and ability to transform challenges into motivation.

The undergraduate basketball career of Magic Johnson at Michigan State University was nothing short of legendary. From 1977 to 1979, he played for the Spartans and made an immediate impact. Magic was renowned for his versatility, basketball IQ, and on the court charisma, all of which he displayed at Michigan State.

In 1979, he led Michigan State to the NCAA championship during his sophomore year. Magic was a triple threat, with the ability to score, grab rebounds, and dole out assists. His performance against Indiana State, lead by Larry Bird, in the championship game was particularly noteworthy. Magic's 24 points, 7 rebounds, and 5 assists contributed to his team securing the championship.

Without question, he was ready for the professional leagues. In 1979, he was drafted by the Los Angeles Lakers.

Early in his NBA tenure, Magic Johnson was faced with a set of obstacles. As the Los Angeles Lakers' first overall selection in the 1979 NBA Draft, he was confronted with enormous expectations. As a rookie, he had to transition from college basketball to the faster and more physical approach of the professional game. Despite being a novice, his leadership position on the team made his circumstance even more extraordinary. Magic had to earn the trust and respect of his more seasoned teammates, which he accomplished through his natural charisma and basketball savvy. In addition, he frequently filled in for injured superstars such as Kareem Abdul-Jabbar-- which required him to assume a bigger role and perform under more pressure. In spite of these early obstacles, Magic Johnson's contagious charisma, versatility, and exceptional basketball IQ enabled him to not only over-come but also surpass these obstacles.

Now, let's dive into one of Magic's most captivating games that created an exhilarating basketball moment. It was Game 6 of the 1980 NBA Finals between the Los Angeles Lakers and the Philadelphia 76ers. It was a championship show-down as the series was deadlocked at 3-3.

The audience was captured by Magic Johnson's broad smile and unbridled confidence. He recognized that this was his opportunity to shine and seized it with both hands. As the game began, he orchestrated the Lakers' offense with the skill of a seasoned pro-- where his dazzling passes left the crowd in astonishment. Magic was not only scoring, but also making his teammates stronger by setting up easy baskets for them.

The game was a high-octane contest, and Magic's enthusiasm inspired the Lakers to play in an aggressive manner that became known as "Showtime." The crowd was on the edge of their seats, and every possession of the ball was electrifying.

However, the outcome hinged on the final few moments. The score was deadlocked, time was running out, and the Lakers desperately needed a miracle. Magic held the ball, and the strain was tremendous. He dribbled, maneuvered past defenders, and launched a delicate hook shot over the towering 76ers with his signature grin. As the ball swished through the net, the Lakers seized the lead!

The arena erupted in applause when Magic Johnson's miraculous shot proved to be the game-winning basket. The Lakers won the game by a score of 123-107 and were subsequently crowned NBA champions. As a rookie, Magic's extraordinary performance was unforgettable. He scored an incredible 42 points, grabbed 15 rebounds, dished out 7 assists, and even made 3 steals. It was a all encompassing display of both his abilities and charisma.

Magic's talents also extend beyond the basketball court into multiple business ventures. As of 2023, he made the Forbes list as 4th athlete billonaire.

Magic Johnson's story is about leadership, teamwork, and the power of a big smile—along his basketball abilities. He demonstrated that regardless of age or experience, anyone with passion, optimism, and hard work can accomplish greatness.

14

OSCAR ROBERTSON - A VICTORY FOR CINCINNATI, 1964

On December 18, 1964, Oscar Robertson prepared to deliver one of the most spectacular performances of his career when he set foot on the basketball court. The Cincinnati Royals were facing the Los Angeles Lakers in a game that would go down in history as one of the most impressive scoring performances.

As soon as the game began, it was evident that something special was happening. Oscar, also known as "Big O," had a fiery nature. He skillfully dribbled, weaved through defenders, and made shots with pinpoint accuracy. No matter how hard the Lakers put up a defense, they were unable to stop him.

Oscar Robertson was born on November 24 1938, in Charlotte, Tennessee, He grew up with a passion for basketball and the desire to play in the NBA.

In his early years as a basketball player, Oscar Robertson encountered a number of obstacles. In the 1940s and 1950s, when he was growing up in a racially segregated America, he encountered discrimination and prejudice due to his race. These social barriers were difficult obstacles, but they only strengthened his will to flourish in the world of basketball.

As Oscar transitioned to college, he attended the University of Cincinnati, where he continued to encounter ethnic segregation—both on and off the court. In those days, African-American collegiate athletes like Oscar had to navigate not only the pressures of college athletics, but also broader social and civil rights issues.

Regardless, Oscar had an exceptional college career and was named to the All American first team three times. During his college days, Oscar scored an average of nearly 34 points per game and leading his team, the Bearcats, to a 79-9 record making it to the Final Four twice. At the time he graduated, Oscar was the all time leading NCAA scorer, taking the Bearcats to national prominence.

In 1960, the Cincinnati Royals selected Oscar with the first overall pick. The process of the NBA Draft during the 1960s was less formal and structured than it is today—when it took place with less media attention.

Oscar was an extraordinary talent on the court, but it wasn't always simple. There were occasions when the Royals struggled to achieve success despite his efforts. These obstacles, however, inspired him to work harder and become a more complete and well-rounded player.

Despite these early obstacles, Oscar Robertson's tenacity, aptitude, and commitment allowed him to become one of the greatest basketball players in history.

During the 1960-61 NBA season, Oscar made an immediate impact on the court where he was named Rookie of the Year. He was renowned for his scoring abilities, versatility and fill up his team's stat sheet with points, rebounds and assists. He was a 12 time NBA All-Star, establishing himself as one basketball's all-time greats.

On a cold December evening in 1964, Oscar Robertson stepped onto the basketball court with the intent of making history. The Cincinnati Royals were scheduled to play the Los Angeles Lakers, but no one was aware that they were about to witness something extraordinary.

From the initial tip off, it was evident that Oscar brought his A-game. He was a basketball wizard who dribbled with dexterity and effortlessly moved around defenders. The Lakers' defense was futile as they were unable to prevent him from scoring. Oscar had the hoop in his crosshairs from every angle on the court that evening.

As the game progressed, it became clear that this was no ordinary performance-- it was an exhibition of scoring. Oscar did not merely score points; he scored them in great succession. Every shot he attempted appeared to end up in the goal. Witnessing a performance that would be talked about for generations, the audience was electrified.

When the final buzzer sounded in the arena, Oscar Robertson had tallied a staggering 56 points. It was a remarkable scoring performance that awed everyone. Not only had he dominated the game, but he had done so in a way that had left a permanent mark.

The "Big O's" 56 points were more than just a number; they demonstrated his extraordinary talent. That December evening etched his legacy as one of basketball's finest scorers in the sport's records forever.

Oscar's performance was motivated by his passion for the game and his ability to improve his colleagues. He was not given the nickname "Big O" for nothing; he had a large heart and a big presence. His performance was driven by his passion for the sport and his ability to make his teammates better. He serves as a reminder that with dedication, practice, and a dash of luck, you can accomplish greatness in your favorite sport.

15

CHARLES BARKLEY - 1993 WESTERN CONFERENCE GAME 7

In the heat of June, Game 7 of the 1993 NBA Western Conference Finals was an epic battle. The Phoenix Suns of Charles Barkley were engaged in a winner-take-all match against the Seattle SuperSonics. The tension in the arena was palpable and the stakes were high.

Barkley was a formidable opponent from the very beginning of the game. He was resolved to lead his team to victory and deliver a ticket to the NBA Finals. Every step he took was poetry in motion. He scored with both power and skill-- leaving the defense dazed by his dexterity.

Charles Barkley is one of the most entertaining and accomplished NBA players of all time. Let's find out why people refer to him as the "Round Mound of Rebound."

Born on February 20 1963, in Leeds, Alabama, Charles Barkley was a big kid with an even bigger personality. But it wasn't just his size that set him on the path to prominence-- it was his passion for basketball.

Early in his life, Charles Barkley encountered a number of obstacles. Growing up in a working-class family in Leeds, Alabama, he faced financial difficulties and a scarcity of training resources. Coming from a poor family, Barkley frequently used improvised hoops to hone his basketball skills. As a child, his size made him an easy target for teasing, but he used these struggles as motivation to become the greatest basketball player possible.

He participated in pickup games against older and tougher opponents, which helped develop his talents. His determination and dedication to the game ultimately lead him to Auburn University, where he emerged as one of the most dominant and exciting collegiate basketball players. From 1981 to 1984, he was a member of the Auburn Tigers and rapidly rose to prominence.

Barkley's college years were marked by his extraordinary athleticism, rebounding prowess, and charismatic personality. He frequently played as an undersized power forward, but his tenacity and talent more than made up for his lack of height. On the court, he was a competitive opponent due to his exceptional trifecta of size, agility, and strength.

During his three years at Auburn, Barkley became a scoring juggernaut, averaging double-digit points and rebounds per game. He was renowned for his vicious dunks, dominating rebounding, and contagious energy. In addition to receiving numerous awards for his performances, he also became a crowd favorite at the games.

Charles Barkley left an undeniable legacy at Auburn despite his relatively short college career. He was named All-American and SEC Player of the Year, and he helped the Tigers reach the NCAA Tournament. His larger-than-life personality paved the way for what was to come next—the NBA.

Charles Barkley's early NBA career was nothing short of spectacular. The Philadelphia 76ers selected him with the fifth overall selection in the 1984 NBA Draft, and he soon became a league sensation.

Despite being shorter than many of his NBA peers at 6 feet and 6 inches, Barkley stands out due to his extraordinary athleticism, incredible rebounding ability, and unparalleled work ethic. On the court, he was a tornado, seizing offensive rebounds and scoring with ease.

In his rookie year, Barkley averaged a double-double with over 14 points and 8.6 rebounds per game. He was named NBA Rookie of the Year as a result. As he progressed through each season, he earned his position among the league's elite players-- making multiple All-Star teams.

Barkley's early NBA years were distinguished by his signature flare and outspoken personality. His charismatic interviews and unfiltered remarks made him a fan favorite. The time he spent with the 76ers marked the beginning of a legendary career.

On June 17, 1992 Barkley was traded from the 76ers to the Phoenix Suns. His arrival had an immediate impact on the team, quickly becoming a franchise favorite. During the 1992-1993 season, he was named MVP, leading the Suns to the Finals.

Game 7 of the 1993 NBA Western Conference Finals was a legendary basketball game. Fans were on the edge of their seats as the Phoenix Suns took on the formidable Seattle SuperSonics.

From the initial tip off, Barkley displayed his extraordinary skills, dribbling with such dexterity that the SuperSonics appeared to be caught in quicksand. Barkley dominated the scoreboard with graceful, pinpoint shots.

His performance, however, was about more than just scoring. He played with passion, and this passion extended to rebounds—where his personal domain became returns. He soared into the air and grabbed each ball as if it were a ticket to the NBA Finals.

At the pinnacle of the game's tension, the score was deadlocked and time was running out. Barkley rose to the challenge. He made a forceful move towards the basket, defying the Sonics' defense, with unflinching determination. As Barkley's basket gave his team the lead, the arena erupted with roaring applause.

The final horn rang, and the Suns came out on top. In the chronicles of NBA history, Game 7 Charles Barkley's remarkable performance left its mark-- he had scored 44 points, grabbed an unbelievable 24 rebounds, and most significantly, led his team to the NBA Finals.

It was a moment that defined Barkley's legacy as a player who thrived under stress and delivered when it counted. His performance in that game was not only about basketball, but also about courage, resolve, and an unrelenting will to win. In the history of basketball, Charles Barkley had penned a chapter that would live on forever.

Charles Barkley's story serves as a reminder that in the world of basketball, personality and perseverance go hand in hand. You may very well be the next "Round Mound of Rebound" if you continue to hone your talents on the court and play with a big heart.

16

STEVE NASH - WESTERN CONFERENCE GAME 6

The sixth game of the 2005 Western Conference Semifinals found the Phoenix Suns and Dallas Mavericks engaged in a fierce battle. The atmosphere in the arena was electric. At the center of it all was Steve Nash, a maestro of the court about to conduction a performance masterpiece.

Prepare to dive into the extraordinary tale of Steve Nash, one of the most exciting and talented NBA basketball players in history. We're about to discover why people refer to him as the "Court Maestro."

Steve Nash was born in Johannesburg, South Africa on February 7, 1974. His family later relocated to Canada, where he developed a passion for sports, particularly soccer. However, he had no idea at the time that he would become a basketball legend.

Steve Nash's path from high school to the NBA was a remarkable one, marked by numerous obstacles and unusual circumstances—with his height being among the most prominent obstacles. At 6 feet 1 inch tall, Nash was considered shorter than many of his basketball contemporaries, particularly forwards and centers. In a sport where height typically provides a significant advantage, Nash had to make up for his lack of stature with exceptional skills and a thorough understanding of the game.

In addition, Steve Nash was raised in Canada, where basketball was less prominent and less-established than in the United States. This limited his exposure to scouts and recruiters when compared to American high school athletes. Therefore, Nash had to work tirelessly to gain recognition on both sides of the border to create a name for himself and earn a college scholarship.

Nash's high school years were characterized by his unwavering dedication to his on court development. He devoted countless hours to honing his dribbling, passing, and shooting accuracy while maintaining excellent grades. This commitment to both academics and athletics would open avenues for him in the future.

Despite the obstacles he faced, Nash was ultimately able to overcome them due to his exceptional work ethic, court vision, and unwavering passion for the game. At Santa Clara University, a relatively modest basketball program, he continued to improve his game and finally attracted the attention of NBA scouts. It was his collegiate accomplishments and commitment during this time that paved the way for his extraordinary NBA career.

Steve Nash went from being a relatively unknown Canadian point guard to one of the league's most exciting and talented players. The Phoenix Suns selected him with the fifteenth overall pick in the first round of the 1996 NBA Draft, where his journey to prominence began.

In his early NBA years, Nash displayed extraordinary ball-handling, court vision, and passing skills. He was a genuine floor general who led his team with both dexterity and accuracy. However, his early career was not free of obstacles-- he battled physical injuries that threatened to impede his advancement. Focusing on recovery, Nash was able to rebound and put himself back on the court.

After a few years with the Suns, Nash was traded to the Dallas Mavericks in 1998. During his time with the team, he established himself as one of the NBA's premiere point guards.

In 2004, Nash returned to the Suns after a brief tenure with the Dallas Mavericks and became the driving force behind their powerful offense. His pick-and-roll plays with forward Amar'e Stoudemire and extraordinary ability to improve his teammates performance were on full display.

In 2005 and 2006, he won consecutive NBA Most Valuable Player awards-- solidifying his position as one of the league's best players.

Game 6 of the 2005 Western Conference Semifinals was a career-defining moment for Steve Nash. His Phoenix Suns were facing his former team, the Dallas Mavericks, in a basketball series that had been a fierce battle.

However, Nash was in complete control of the game from the initial tip-off. His dribbling skills were as on point, allowing him to control the ball with precision. His court vision was unparalleled, as he delivered passes that appeared to have their own eyes and found his teammates with pinpoint accuracy.

During this game, Dirk Nowitzki led the Mavericks in a valiant effort, but Nash was determined to lead his Suns to victory. With every dribble, pass, and shot, he displayed an extraordinary basketball IQ. As the game continued, it became increasingly tense. The Suns were falling behind, and time was running out. Nash found himself in possession of the ball with mere seconds remaining. The arena held its breath as he suddenly launched a long-range three-pointer.

The ball entered the net, tying the score and sending the game into overtime.

Nash continued to direct the Suns' offense in overtime, setting up his colleagues and making crucial plays—where the Suns had secured the victory at the final moment. Nash's performance was nothing short of legendary. He finished the game with 39 points, 12 assists, and a memorable game-tying three-pointer.

Game 6 of the 2005 Western Conference Semifinals was a testament to Steve Nash's extraordinary talents, leadership, and fierce competitiveness. This game demonstrated why he was considered one of the greatest point guards in NBA history.

The journey of Steve Nash is an inspiring story of perseverance and tenacity, demonstrating that with hard work and a profound passion for one's craft, it is possible to overcome even the most challenging obstacles and achieve greatness in a competitive field. With practice, you too could become the next "Maestro of the Court"!

17

STEPH CURRY - THE WARRIORS BOUNCE BACK, MAY 28 2015

O n May 27, 2015, Stephen Curry, nicknamed "Splash Brother," delivered a performance that will live on in NBA history. It was Game 5 of the Western Conference Finals, and the Golden State Warriors and Houston Rockets were in a heated face off of epic proportions. It was a game where Curry was about to demonstrate his magic to the world.

Prepare to step into the extraordinary story of Stephen Curry, one of the most electrifying NBA players of all time. We're about to discover why he is known as the "Splash Brother."

Stephen Curry, also known as Steph, was born in Akron, Ohio, on March 14, 1988. Basketball was in his genes, as his father, Dell Curry, was also an NBA player.

Stephen Curry began exhibiting his extraordinary basketball aptitude during his high school years at Charlotte Christian School in North Carolina. Despite his short stature, he demonstrated an exceptional work ethic and a profound love for the game. His abilities, especially his ball-handling and long-distance shooting, were already developing quickly. Curry's dedication and determination were evident, despite his lack of popularity as a recruit. He led his high school team to an impressive 32-5 record in his senior year, foreshadowing his future success.

Curry continued to surpass expectations at Davidson College, where he transferred from high school. As a member of the Davidson Wildcats, he rapidly rose to fame in college basketball. In his sophomore season, he had a remarkable NCAA Tournament run that won the adoration of fans across the nation. His exceptional three-point marksmanship and ability to carry his team deep into the tournament catapulted him to prominence. During his sophomore year, when he led the NCAA in scoring, Curry solidified his reputation as one of the best shooters in college basketball. These college years were crucial in displaying Curry's talent and establishing the groundwork for his successful NBA career.

On June 25, 2009, Stephen Curry was drafted into the NBA-- the Golden State Warriors selected him with the seventh overall selection in the first round of the 2009 NBA Draft. This draft marked the beginning of Curry's professional career, and at the time, no one could have predicted that he would become one of the finest shooters and players in the NBA.

Early in his career, Stephen Curry encountered a number of obstacles that tested his will on the road to NBA stardom. His size and stamina represented one of the biggest obstacles. Curry was not the most physically imposing player, and his relatively shorter stature raised doubts about his ability to compete with opponents of greater size and strength. To combat this, he engaged in rigorous strength and conditioning training in order to withstand the physical demands of the professional league.

The threat of injury was another significant obstacle Curry had to overcome. Early in his NBA career, he struggled with recurring ankle injuries, which not only hindered his performance but also raised questions about his durability. To overcome these setbacks and keep his career on track, he underwent multiple surgeries and intensive rehabilitation.

Beyond physical obstacles, Curry had to demonstrate his worth on the court. Despite his outstanding collegiate career at Davidson, he was not a highly touted NBA prospect, and there were doubts as to whether his distinctive college playing style would translate to the professional level. Because of this, he had to prove that he belonged among NBA's elite. With this, Curry's defensive abilities were also criticized. This perception of him as a defensive threat drove him to improve his defensive abilities and become a more well-rounded player.

Playing for the Warriors, team success did not occur overnight. Before becoming the dominant force they are today, the Golden State Warriors endured several difficult seasons. Curry endured periods of playing with losing records, but he and his teammates ultimately achieved the championship success that has defined his extraordinary career.

Stephen Curry surmounted these early obstacles to become one of the greatest shooters and point guards in NBA history by utilizing his unwavering determination, tireless work ethic, and unshakeable confidence in his skills. His journey exemplifies the significance of perseverance in the pursuit of one's dreams.

The term "Splash" in "Splash Brothers" refers to the sound a basketball produces when it passes through the hoop after a successful long shot-- especially from the three-point line. Fans and commentators nicknamed Curry and Klay Thompson the "Splash Brothers" due to their ability to make three-pointers consistently and frequently in spectacular fashion.

In addition to redefining the game, their combined long-range shooting prowess has been a crucial factor in the Golden State Warriors' success over the years, resulting in multiple NBA championships.

On the evening of May 27, 2015, Stephen Curry participated in a historic basketball game. It was Game 5 of the Western

Conference Finals, and the Golden State Warriors and Houston Rockets were engaged in a fierce conflict.

From the opening tip off, Curry displayed his basketball wizardry. His coordinated dribbling left defenders bewildered, and he appeared to have an unbreakable connection with the ball. But what truly set him apart was his long-range shooting ability. He had the exceptional ability to make three-point shots from distances that most players would not even attempt.

In the heat of the battle, the Rockets were intent on containing Curry, but he was in the zone. Shot after shot, he sent the basketball arcing through the air-- each one landing with astonishing accuracy. Spectators from around the world watched in awe.

As the game neared its end, the score was deadlocked and the stakes were at their highest. With only seconds remaining, Curry gained possession of the ball. The entire arena held its breath in anticipation of his next move. A rapid step back and a flick of the wrist sent the basketball soaring through the air, where it hovered before falling gracefully through the net.

When the final buzzer sounded, the Warriors had prevailed, and Curry's performance was inscribed into the history books. That night, he scored 26 points-- including several jaw-dropping three-pointers and his final shot.

Stephen Curry's performance in Game 5 of the 2015 Western Conference Finals was a demonstration of his skill, precision, and ability to perform under the biggest arena. It was a night in which he demonstrated a special kind of magic on the court-- living up to his nickname, "Splash Brother."

Steph Curry was not only known for his incredible shooting; but also for his cooperation, humility, and enthusiasm for the game. He demonstrated that through hard work and a fearless attitude, greatness can be attained.

So keep practicing your three-point shots, and who knows-- maybe one day you'll become the next "Splash Brother"!

18

MOSES MALONE - 1983 FINALS GAME 4

In the summer of 1983, the entire basketball world is watching Game 4 of the 1983 NBA Finals as the Philadelphia 76ers are face off against the fierce Los Angeles Lakers. However, all eyes are on the 76ers "Chairman of the Boards", Moses Malone who is on fire setting up his team for victory.

From the initial tip off, Malone asserts his authority. As if possessing a special instinct for where the ball will land, he swoops in like a hawk to grab offensive rebounds. With each play, he revitalizes his team's offense by generating second and third scoring opportunities— giving a performance for the ages.

Moses Malone was born in Petersburg, Virginia on March 23, 1955. On the basketball court, he wasn't a flashy sensation, but a force to be reckoned with. Even from a young age, he displayed extraordinary talent for the sport.

Malone was raised in a modest, disadvantaged community where he learned the value of perseverance and hard work as his family often struggled to make ends meet. To help support his family, he performed odd jobs such as picking potatoes in the fields and shining shoes. These early experiences instilled in him a profound appreciation for the value of tenacity in the face of challenges.

His family's financial struggles also compounded his academic difficulties. As a result, Moses chose to leave Petersburg High School prior to finishing his senior year. This decisive choice marked the beginning of his extraordinary journey. Unlike many of his classmates who opted for college, decided to pursue a professional basketball career directly after high school.

However, this decision was not without obstacles and uncertainties. During his era of professional basketball, the transition from high school to the NBA was less common-- and it was accompanied by skepticism and uncertainty by many league scouts. Because of this, Moses Malone was required to demonstrate not only his preparedness for the NBA, but also his ability to excel at the highest levels of the sport with seasoned players.

The Portland Trail Blazers selected him with the fifth overall selection in the 1974 ABA-NBA Draft, but later traded him to the Buffalo Braves. However, he did not play a single game for the Braves-- his NBA career began, in fact, in 1976 when he joined the Houston Rockets.

Moses Malone was unmistakably exceptional from the moment he set foot on an NBA court. He possessed an extraordinary work ethic, an unrelenting drive, and an exceptional ability to dominate the game. His tenacity on the rebound boards, which earned him the title "Chairman of the Boards," was unmatched. He consistently led the league in this vital statistical, demonstrating a powerful knack for recovering offensive rebounds.

Malone's ability to score was also remarkable. He had an unmatched touch around the rim and a talent for putting the ball in the net. Whether he scored in the post, from mid-range jumpers, or by converting offensive rebounds into second-chance points—Malone was also a scoring juggernaut.

In 1979, he led the Houston Rockets to the NBA Finals and was dubbed MVP of the league. His influence on the sport was unmistakable, and he was renowned for his court leadership.

One of Moses Malone's most captivating games was with the Philadelphia 76ers in the fourth game of the 1983 NBA Finals. They were competing against the fiercely competitive Los Angeles Lakers-- whose roster included basketball greats such as Magic Johnson and Kareem Abdul-Jabbar.

Malone's presence was felt right from the opening tip off. He was a magnet for offensive rebounds, consuming blundered shots as if they were his own personal treasure. It appeared that he had a special connection with the basketball, as he knew exactly where each shot would strike. Moses gave the 76ers more and more scoring opportunities with every rebound he grabbed.

As the game neared its end, the score was close and the tension was knife-thick. With seconds remaining on the clock, Moses found himself under the basket, where he thrived. He grabbed a crucial offensive rebound and drove the ball through the net with pure determination. The 76ers seized the lead, prompting thunderous applause from the crowd.

When the final buzzer sounded, it was evident that the 76ers had prevailed-- and Moses Malone was the night's hero!

He had recorded an impressive 24 points and, even more astonishingly, an incredible 23 rebounds. He demonstrated to the world why he was known as the "Chairman of the Boards" in the game's final minutes.

The performance of Moses Malone was a model of basketball excellence. It demonstrated his ability to dominate the game.

Moses Malone's life serves as an illuminating and motivational example of how a person's unwavering commitment to their ambitions, combined with perseverance and hard work, can lead to extraordinary success despite humble beginnings.

19

DAVID ROBINSON - A 71 POINT GAME ON APRIL 24, 1994

In the final game of the NBA regular season on April 24, 1994, the San Antonio Spurs were competing against the Los Angeles Clippers. The Spurs' star center David Robinson, nicknamed "The Admiral," was responsible for one of the greatest individual basketball performances ever. Prepare for an remarkable journey through his life and an exciting play-by-play of one of his most memorable games.

Born on August 6th 1965, in Key West, Florida, David Robinson grew up to be a scholar-athlete in addition to being a basketball champion. He attended the United States Naval Academy, where he combined his passion for basketball and commitment to serving his country.

His family's frequent relocations as a result of his father's Navy career was one of the most difficult obstacles he faced. This constant relocation made it difficult to establish roots and cultivate enduring friendships. In addition, Robinson experienced a growth spurt in high school, which caused struggles with coordination and made him more critical of his athletic abilities. Even more so, on the basketball court, this made it difficult to compete with more seasoned players.

Nonetheless, Robinson's unwavering dedication to his dreams enabled him to surmount these early obstacles. He decided to enroll at the United States Naval Academy-- combining his passion for basketball with his sense of duty to serve his country. This decision meant he had to adhere to rigorous military discipline and a demanding academic schedule. However, during his final two years, Robinson made All-American and was awarded the Naismith and Wooden awards.

David Robinson's early days in the NBA were marked by the anticipation of his arrival and the rapid metamorphosis of the San Antonio Spurs into a feared competitor. Robinson was prepared to leave his mark on the league after being selected first overall in the NBA Draft of 1987.

His NBA debut, however, was delayed. Robinson had unfulfilled obligations to the United States Navy when he was conscripted. Two years after being drafted, he entered the NBA in the 1989-1990 season. This meant that Robinson was older than the most NBA rookies when he made his debut.

Robinson's exceptional talent became apparent once he assumed the Spurs' uniform. His athleticism, combined with his towering stature and shot-blocking skills, made him an instant defensive standout. During the 1989-1990 NBA season, he was named Rookie of the Year, echoing his impact on the court.

Even more so, Robinson's offensive game evolved quickly. Not only was he a feared defensive force, but he was also an exceptional scorer. With his speed and deftness around the rim, he became one of the league's best centers.

By the end of his second season, Robinson had established himself as a dominant force, garnering the moniker "The Admiral"-- attributed to his time at the Naval Academy, as well as, his dominating presence on the court. Due to his exceptional skills and leadership, the Spurs went from a struggling team to a major NBA contender.

Robinson's force was felt on the 24th of April, 1994. The San Antonio Spurs were taking on the Los Angeles Clippers, and on that fateful day, "The Admiral," was about to make history in a manner that few players ever do.

Robinson was on a mission from the time he tipped the ball. Not only was he dominant, but he was also unstoppable. Each time he handled the ball, it appeared destined to enter the hoop. He scored from all over the court-- whether through dunks in the paint or jumpers from the perimeter.

Robinson's brilliance was not limited to scoring, however. On the offensive glass, he seized rebounds with authority. Likewise, on the defensive end, he guarded the basket with ferocity, deflecting the Clippers' attempts at scoring with ease.

The Spurs realized as the game progressed that something extraordinary was happening. They continued to pass the ball to Robinson, and he continued to deliver. The audience's astonishment grew as his game point total continued to rise. The tension grew electrifying as they watched history being made.

When the final buzzer sounded, David Robinson had accomplished the impossible. He scored a remarkable 71 points, collected 14 rebounds, and even had time for two blocks. Robinson's name was etched into the record books after the San Antonio Spurs won the game. His 71-point game remains one of the most impressive performances in NBA history.

As of this book, Robinson is only one of eight players to achieve 70 or more points in a single game.

David Robinson's rise from a scholar-athlete at the Naval Academy to one of the most dominant centers in NBA history is a testimony to hard work, devotion, and a dedication to excellence. His legacy as "The Admiral" will forever be remembered in NBA lore for showing that excellence can be attained-- both on and off the court.

20

DWYANE WADE - 2006 NBA FINALS GAME 3

O n June 13, 2006, the entire basketball community is glued to their televisions to watch the NBA Finals. On this night, Dwyane Wade, nicknamed "Flash" is about to steal the show with his electrifying speed and on court skills. It is Game 3 of the NBA Finals and the Miami Heat face the Dallas Mavericks, in urgent need a victory. The pressure is enormous, and the arena is teeming with anticipation. From the time the game begins, Wade dominates the court like a hurricane, approaching the rim with the fierce determination of a lion on the prowl.

Dwyane Tyrone Wade Jr. was born in Chicago, Illinois on January 17, 1982. Growing up on the rough South Side of Chicago, his journey to becoming an NBA superstar from humble beginnings was nothing short of remarkable.

Dwyane fell in love with basketball at a young age, using the sport as a retreat from the difficulties of his neighborhood. He honed his skills on playgrounds and in the gym-- aspiring one day to play in the big league.

Wade's early life exemplified his extraordinary resilience and unbreakable spirit. Growing up on the South Side of Chicago, he was constantly confronted with challenges and adversity as the community was frequently characterized by poverty, crime, and limited opportunities.

To make matters worse, the marriage between Wade's parents ended when he was only a few months old. He was raised by his mother, Jolinda Wade. Like many other single-parent households, Wade's family experienced financial difficulties, making it a daily struggle to make ends meet.

But despite these challenges, young Dwyane discovered his passion: basketball. The neighborhood courts and play-grounds served as his refuge from his community's troubles. Here, he refined his skills, diligently practiced, and envisioned a brighter future through the sport he cherished.

Wade's path to success, however, wasn't easy. During his senior year of high school, he encountered academic difficulties that at times appeared to threaten his admission into collegiate basketball. However, his unyielding will drove him forward and with the assistance of mentors, instructors, and his mother, he was able to enroll at Marquette University.

Wade excelled both on and off the court at Marquette. His undergraduate years at Marquette University were pivotal in his path to NBA superstardom. He demonstrated that, in addition to being an outstanding athlete, he was also a dedicated and focused student. His undergraduate accomplishments paved the way for his extraordinary journey to the NBA.

On the court, Wade was nothing less than extraordinary. In the NCAA tournament, he led Marquette to the Final Four-- an incredible accomplishment for the university. His skills and leadership on the court attracted the attention of NBA scouts, and his draft status began to rise.

Wade made the choice to enter the NBA Draft after his junior year at Marquette. The Miami Heat selected him with the fifth overall selection in the 2003 NBA Draft after making a pivotal decision. This marked the beginning of his NBA career, where he would go on to become one of the league's most iconic figures.

Now, let's fast forward a few years to one of his most epic games.

In Game 3 of the NBA Finals, the Miami Heat and the Dallas Mavericks face off. The Heat are two games behind and desperate for a victory.

As the game begins, it is evident that Wade is a formidable opponent. He is not merely playing; he is dancing with the ball, creating a flurry of energy toward the basket. With layup after layup, he leaves the Dallas defense in disbelief with his dexterity.

However, Wade is not only a scorer-- he is also a playmaker. He orchestrates the offense for the Heat by passing to colleagues with pinpoint accuracy. And when necessary, he snatches offensive rebounds with the determination of a seasoned center.

The game develops into a vicious struggle for control of the board, but Wade shines brightest. He is in his element, even though the score is deadlocked. The audience is on the edge of their seats--this is the type of moment from which legends are produced.

With only seconds remaining, Wade has possession of the ball. He takes a stride back, shoots a three-pointer, and then, time suddenly freezes.

Silence, and then -- the swish of the net!

It is music to the ears of the Miami crowd, which erupt in jubilation. The game has ended in the most dramatic fashion due to Wade's shot.

Dwyane Wade recorded an astounding 42 points, 13 rebounds, and 2 assists by the final buzzer. The Miami Heat have finally won their first NBA Finals game of the season, and Wade's name will forever remembered.

Dwyane Wade's journey the rough streets of Chicago to NBA superstardom is an inspiring tale of perseverance and effort. His ability to rise to the occasion in critical games established him as a genuine basketball icon. His legacy will eternally inspire aspiring ballplayers to reach the major leagues.

21

SCOTTIE PIPPEN- A SHOWDOWN IN CHICAGO

O n a frigid evening in Chicago on February 18, 1997, the United Center is buzzing with anticipation as the Chicago Bulls prepare to take on the Denver Nuggets. Scottie Pippen, the Bulls' versatile star, is preparing for a night that will go down in NBA history among a sea of basketball fans. One of the greatest wingmen in the game was about to leave an indelible mark.

Scottie Pippen, who was born in Hamburg, Arkansas on September 25, 1965, had a unique path to NBA stardom. Pippen was a tall, slender child who enjoyed playing basketball—a passion that would eventually inspire him to become one of the Chicago Bulls' all-time greats.

Pippen's early days was a story of determination and tenacity. Having been born into a modest family in Hamburg,

Arkansas, his family confronted financial hardships, but he never allowed these obstacles to hold him back.

Growing up in a rural town, teenage athletes had few opportunities. In high school, Pippen's talent frequently went unnoticed despite his towering stature. He was not a highly recruited player, and he did not receive significant college scholarship offers. However, he was not deterred.

Instead, he took his basketball talents and dreams to the smaller University of Central Arkansas, where he played college basketball. There, he had the opportunity to shine and improve his game. His diligence and perseverance eventually drew the attention of NBA scouts, who could no longer deny his level of playing.

Scottie Pippen's transition from the University of Central Arkansas to the beginning of his NBA career is a remarkable journey that highlights his aptitude and perseverance. Pippen was eligible for the NBA Draft following his college years, and it was during this crucial period that he took a significant step toward basketball greatest.

The path that led Pippen from a smaller institution to the NBA was not without challenges. He entered the 1987 NBA Draft and was selected fifth overall by the Seattle SuperSonics. However, in a shocking turn of events, he was transferred to the Chicago Bulls shortly thereafter. This signaled the start of his partnership with Michael Jordan and the Bulls' rise to NBA dominance.

Pippen had to adjust to the high level of competition and the fast pace of professional basketball early on. He swiftly adapted to the Bulls' system and became a crucial component to the team's success. During the 1990s, Pippen's defensive prowess, versatility, and ability to contribute on both ends of the court were instrumental in the Bulls securing six NBA championships.

Of course, this success occurred after he joined forces with the legendary Michael Jordan to create one of the most legendary duos in NBA history.

Pippen's full powers were on display one night in February of 1997, when the Chicago Bulls are playing the Denver Nuggets. The United Center is buzzing with excitement as fans eagerly fill the arena in anticipation of an unforgettable basketball matchup.

The dynamic and versatile hero of the Bulls, Scottie Pippen, is about to deliver a performance for the ages. As the game gets underway, it is immediately clear that Pippen is in the zone and prepared to light up the court. He steals the ball, disrupts plays, and defends with unmatched ferocity.

Pippen assaults the basket with grace and accuracy, sinking layups and mid-range jumpers. Equally remarkable is his ability to create opportunities for his Bulls teammates to land their own shots while racking up assists.

Pippen's influence increases with each passing minute as the game progresses. He orchestrates each play with the finesse and flair of a conductor leading an orchestra. Each pass, theft, and basket is like a note in a symphony of basketball.

Pippen seizes the opportunity with the score tied and the game on the line. In the final seconds of the game, he methodically sinks a crucial three-pointer, breaking the tie and giving the Bulls the lead. As the final buzzer sounds, the audience roars with excitement.

Scottie Pippen is the undisputed hero of the evening as the Chicago Bulls emerge victorious with a final score of 134–123. As the game's undisputed MVP, Pippen's 47 points leaves everyone in admiration of his extraordinary performance.

This game against the Denver Nugget displayed Scottie Pippen's basketball brilliance in full form-- His incredible scoring, defensive prowess, and leadership made him one of the NBA's finest players.

Scottie Pippen's rise to NBA superstardom from a small town in Arkansas is an inspiring story of talent, teamwork, and perseverance. Even the greatest players rely on their teammates to achieve success.

22

JERRY WEST - JAN 17 1962

The year was 1962 and the Lakers and Knicks squared off in a historic matchup at the Los Angeles Memorial Sports Arena, Jerry West, one of the NBA's all-time greats, was expected to deliver an unforgettable performance, and the crowd was reeling with anticipation.

Jerry West, born in Chelyan, West Virginia on May 28, 1938, had an extraordinary journey from a small town to NBA prominence. As a kid, basketball was his favorite sport-- however, he had no idea that his passion for basketball would lead him to the NBA.

West grew up during a period of economic hardship due to the decline of the coal mining industry. This meant that he grew up in an environment with limited financial resources, which many families, including his own, endured during the Great Depression.

As a youth, Jerry West's family was struck by tragedy when David, his older brother who served in the military, tragically died during the Korean War. This loss profoundly affected young Jerry and he felt a profound sense of duty to honor his brother's memory and make the most of the opportunities that life presented him.

While West displayed early promise in basketball, he confronted an additional obstacle-- limited exposure to a high level basketball competition in his small town. As a result of this, he was not heavily recruited by colleges, and received few scholarship offers.

Despite these obstacles, Jerry West's upbringing instilled in him a tenacious work ethic and an unyielding will to push through adversity. His rise to NBA greatness was fueled by the memory of his brother and his passion for basketball.

West eventually played college basketball at West Virginia University, where he acquired the nickname "Mr. Clutch" due to his ability to make clutch plays.

During his college career, West achieved a total of 2,309 points with 1240 rebounds, signaling a future NBA legend in the making. West's tenacity so was intense during playing, that he famously broke his nose during a game against the Kentucky Wildcats and led his team to victory all while breathing through his mouth.

Outside of college, West co-captained the US men's basketball team with Oscar Robertson. Together they would lead the team to a gold medal in the 1960 Summer Olympics.

As fate would have it, the 1960 NBA Draft came calling and his professional career began.

NBA scouts took note of West's college success. He was selected second overall by the Minneapolis Lakers in the 1960 NBA Draft. The team relocated to Los Angeles and changed its name to the Los Angeles Lakers shortly thereafter.

His early years in the NBA were marked by outstanding individual and team success. West soon became one of the league's top talents-- known for his versatility as a scorer and persistent defender.

Despite confronting feared opponents such as the Boston Celtics in the 1960s, West's Lakers qualified for multiple NBA Finals. Despite facing strong opposition, the Lakers' triumph was largely due to West's outstanding performance.

On January 17, 1962, the Los Angeles Lakers and the New York Knicks were set to play an exciting game at the Los Angeles Memorial Sports Arena where Jerry West was about to deliver one of the most extraordinary performances in NBA history.

It was clear that West was on a mission from the opening tip-off. He dribbled gracefully down the court, demonstrating his superior ball-handling aptitude. His jump shots were like poetry in motion, gliding through the net with amazing accuracy. As West continued to rack up points, the Knicks' defense struggled to slow him down.

West's brilliance extended past scoring-- he set up his colleagues with pinpoint passes and created remarkable scoring opportunities. Equally impressive on the defensive end, he made steals and grabbed crucial rebounds.

As the game's climax grew closer, the Lakers and Knicks were engaged in a tight battle. With seconds remaining on the clock and the Lakers down by one point, the stress was on. Jerry West quickly became the center of attention. He received the inbound pass, dribbled up the court, and made a jump shot at the buzzer with the composure of a seasoned veteran.

As the Lakers celebrated a 129-121 victory, the audience at the Los Angeles Memorial Sports Arena fell into stunned silence. Jerry West's 63-point performance cemented his place in NBA history. His scoring, playmaking, and decisive performance in that game stand as an enduring moment of basketball greatness.

Jerry West's rise from a small town in West Virginia to NBA superstardom is an inspiring tale of talent, commitment, and the ability to perform under stress. His moments on the court continue to serve as an inspiration for young ballers everywhere. With hard work and talent, you too, can achieve glory on the court and in life.

23

KEVIN GARNETT - 2008 NBA FINALS KING

The pressure was on during the 2008 NBA Finals. In a fiercely fought battle, power forward Kevin Garnett was determined to lead his Boston Celtics to regain their position as the best basketball team in the NBA.

However, Garnett's path to the Finals was not simple. From his early days in Minnesota to the momentous trade that brought him to Boston, he endured years of ups and downs. However, during the 2008 Finals, he was on the brink of greatness.

Prepare to dive into the incredible story of Kevin Garnett, one of the NBA's most iconic athletes.

Kevin Garnett, who was born in Mauldin, South Carolina, on May 19, 1976, had an extraordinary journey from a small town to NBA prominence. On and off the court, he was a towering figure known for his intensity, dedication, and all-encompassing skills.

Early challenges in Kevin Garnett's life helped mold him into the legendary NBA player he became. Growing up in a modest, working-class household, Garnett's family confronted financial challenges and had to learn early on the importance of perseverance and hard work.

His height was another significant obstacles he encountered. During middle school, he reached a height of 6 feet 7 inches, which made him stand out in a crowd. On the basketball court, his height also carried with it high expectations and pressure-- but it also made it difficult for him to fit in socially.

Despite these challenges, Garnett found refuge in basketball. It became evident that he had a talent for the game, and he worked relentlessly to improve his skills. He attended Mauldin High School, where he established himself as an outstanding basketball prospect.

Garnett's decision to enter the 1995 NBA Draft directly from high school was a critical event in his life. He had become one of the first players to do so in 20 years—making this decision fraught with apprehension since it was a path less frequently taken. However, Garnett's extraordinary work ethic, talent, and determination paid off, as the Minnesota Timberwolves selected him with the fifth overall selection.

Early in his NBA career, Kevin Garnett enjoyed unrivaled individual success and strong dedication to his craft. After becoming part of the Minnesota Timberwolves, Garnett rapidly established himself as one of the league's most promising young players. His work ethic was on full display during his time as he was a versatile, nimble power forward who excelled at scoring, rebounding, and defense. Garnett became an NBA All-Star and one of the league's most dominant athletes.

Despite his exceptional performance as a rookie player, Garnett failed to win a championship in his early career. Despite numerous opportunities, the Timberwolves were unable to capture the title. This lack of team success weighed heavily on Garnett-- who yearned to win an NBA title.

Throughout this period, Garnett's dedication to improving his game and his leadership on and off the court were unwavering. The championship ring he desired, however, still remained just out of reach.

However, in 2007 Garnett's fortunes improved. He was traded to the Boston Celtics, where he joined Ray Allen and Paul Pierce to form the "Big Three." In his first season with the Celtics, Garnett realized his long-held championship aspiration-- where his tenure was forever defined by Boston's 2008 NBA Finals victory.

The stage was set for the 2008 NBA Finals, and Kevin Garnett's Boston Celtics were determined to reclaim their position as the best basketball team in the world.

A best-of-six series between the Boston Celtics and the Los Angeles Lakers would crown the NBA champion. Garnett, along with fellow "Big Three" superstars were on a mission to restore Boston's grandeur.

Garnett's influence throughout the series was unmistakable. His defensive drive, shot-blocking skills, and rebounding prowess set the tone for the Celtics. He was an intimidating presence on the court, making it virtually impossible for the Lakers to score close to the basket.

Garnett's performance reached its peak as the final seconds ticked away. He made jump shots, made crucial defensive stops, and made the type of clutch plays upon which championships are won. In Game 6, he tallied 26 points and grabbed 14 rebounds, leaving his mark on the scorecard.

When the final buzzer sounded, the Boston Celtics were crowned NBA champions-- largely due to Kevin Garnett's unwavering dedication and remarkable performance throughout the series. It was a defining moment in Garnett's legendary career and evidence of his ability to rise to the occasion on basketball's grandest stage.

Kevin Garnett had secured the championship ring he had been working so hard to achieve.

Kevin Garnett's journey in the 2008 NBA Finals is a reminder to young sports fans that commitment, teamwork, and never giving up in the face of adversity can lead to the ultimate victory. Garnett's legacy lives on as a shining example of what it means to be a champion in the NBA.

24

ELGIN BAYLOR - 1962 FINALS GAME 7

The seventh game of the 1962 NBA Finals was a moment in basketball history that will live on forever, and forward Elgin Baylor was at the center of it all. His Los Angeles Lakers were competing against their regular rivals, the Boston Celtics, in a game that would come to define an era.

Elgin Baylor was born in Washington, D.C., on September 16, 1934. It was evident from a young age that he had a special connection with basketball. On the courts of Washington, D.C., he refined his skills by performing gravity-defying dunks and making defenders dizzy with his incredible moves. Elgin Baylor's path to NBA stardom was marked by early adversity that he overcame with determination. Growing up during the racially segregated United States of the 1940s and '50s, Baylor confronted significant obstacles, especially in pursuing his passion for basketball.

Baylor attended an all-black high school, where he honed his basketball skills, but racial segregation limited his opportunities for widespread recognition and exposure. Despite this, his talent on the court was readily apparent and he became a local sensation in the DC area very quickly.

After graduating high school, Baylor confronted another obstacle-- limited opportunities for black basketball players in college. The discrimination he faced as a student at the College of Idaho made his college experience more difficult. However, he transferred to Seattle University, where he discovered an environment more receptive to his athletic abilities.

His time there was highlighted by outstanding basketball performances, and he quickly became one of the country's most dominant collegiate athletes. During his senior year, Baylor averaged an impressive 32.5 points and 19.3 rebounds per game, demonstrating his extraordinary versatility and scoring ability. In 1958, despite losing to the University of Kentucky, he was selected as an All-American and led his team to the NCAA championship.

Elgin Baylor was selected first overall in the 1958 NBA Draft by the Minneapolis Lakers-- a team that subsequently relocated to Los Angeles. This was a pivotal moment in his career, as he was one of the first players to make the transition directly from college to the NBA. The entrance of

Baylor into the league was met with much anticipation and enthusiasm.

His early days in the NBA were marked by a series of extraordinary accomplishments. In the 1958-59 season, Baylor was awarded the Rookie of the Year. He became renowned for his scoring ability and on the court techniques. Fans were impressed by Baylor's acrobatic moves and offensive skills, which made him one of the NBA's top performers.

While Baylor attained individual success early in his career, he was unable to win an NBA championship. In 1972, near the end of his playing career with the Los Angeles Lakers, he finally won a championship-- despite having a few near misses.

One of Elgin Baylor's most captivating games occurred at the 1962 NBA Finals. Baylor's Lakers were competing against the NBA's dominant team, the Boston Celtics. The series was tied at 3-3, making Game 7 an epic showdown. The Lakers were aware that they faced a fierce challenge, but Baylor, with his extraordinary talent and determination, was intent on leaving his mark.

From the tip off, Baylor was on fire. The gravity-defying grace with which he executed dunks, mid-range jumpers, and driving layups made them appear effortless. The hard-hitting defense of the Celtics was unable to contain him.

Baylor maneuvered and threaded through defenders while firing shot after shot. His point total continued to rise, and it became evident that something genuinely extraordinary was happening.

As the clock was winding down, the legendary Celtics defense were hurling everything they had at Baylor-- but he appeared to be unstoppable.

As the final buzzer sounded, Elgin Baylor had tallied an astounding 41 points in a single game.

The Lakers narrowly lost that game to the Celtics despite Baylor's historic performance, but his legacy was permanently left on the court. He had shown the world what a single player with talent and determination could accomplish and his stats reflected it.

Elgin Baylor's performance in Game 7 of the 1962 NBA Finals is a shining illustration of the basketball court's magical potential. His name is etched indelibly into the NBA record books, serving as a symbol of excellence and an inspiration to all aspiring young basketball players.

25

CHRIS PAUL - DECEMBER 7, 2007

The evening of December 7, 2007 will be eternally imprinted in the minds of basketball fans, as point guard Chris Paul orchestrated a display of pure magic. On that night, his New Orleans Hornets faced the Utah Jazz in a game that turned into an epic overtime battle.

Chris Paul is one of the finest point guards to ever grace the game of basketball. Born in Lewisville, North Carolina, on May 6, 1985, Chris Paul had a basketball in his palms before he could walk. His court skills were readily apparent at an early age.

As a student at North Carolina's West Forsyth School, Paul quickly gained a reputation as a basketball prodigy. His court abilities were indisputable, and he was regarded as one of the best high school athletes in the nation. However, just as he was establishing a name for himself in the basketball community-- tragedy struck.

Paul received devastating news the summer before his senior year-- Nathaniel Jones, his cherished grandfather, was tragically killed. This event shook Paul to his core and forever changed his life. Nathaniel Jones had been a major influence on Paul's life, establishing in him the importance of diligence, discipline, and perseverance.

Paul used the tragedy as a source of motivation as opposed to living in grief. He dedicated his basketball performances to his late grandfather in order to channel his emotions. Each time he stepped onto the court, he played with a energy and drive that transcended the game.

During his senior year, Paul scored an incredible 61 points in a single game, garnering him widespread attention. By the time he completed the season, he averaged just over 30 points per game and led West Forsyth to the Class 4A Eastern Regional Finals.

Paul's success in high school was a testament to his resilience and ability to use adversity as motivation. His journey from high school to the NBA was distinguished by his dedication to the game, fueled by his grandfather's memory.

Chris Paul played for Wake Forest University were he set new records for a freshman, where he was named ACC Rookie of the Year. He continued playing with consistent scoring through 2005.

Paul's road to the NBA was paved with grit, determination and a touch of magic. After excelling in high school and college, he was drafted by the New Orleans Hornets with the fourth overall selection in 2005. From that point on, the league knew it had brought on an exceptional talent.

Paul's superior basketball IQ and court vision were immediately apparent. His ability to control the tempo of the game and create scoring opportunities for his teammates made him a standout player.

During his early days in the NBA, Paul's training regimen was grueling. His work ethic and commitment to developing involved countless hours spent honing his ball-handling, shooting, and defensive skills on the court. In order to endure the rigorous NBA schedule, he concentrated on increasing his strength and conditioning. Paul's basketball intelligence was enhanced through video playback analysis, in addition to his physical training. He would analyze the strategies of his opponents, study game footage, and constantly seek methods to out maneuver his opponents.

This commitment to the physical and mental aspects of the game enabled him to excel early in his NBA career-- garnering him multiple All-Star nods and a reputation as one of the league's best point guards.

The 7th of December, 2007 was a date that would soon be inscribed into NBA record books. Chris Paul was about to lead his team into a lively overtime matchup against the Utah Jazz.

As the arena buzzed with excitement, the stage was set for an epic showdown.

From the opening tip off, Chris Paul dominated the game. With his lightning-fast crossovers and pinpoint passes, he resembled a basketball ace, controlling every action on the court. Paul orchestrated the Hornets' offense with a deftness that left the Jazz chasing shadows.

Chris Paul seized control of the game with just seconds remaining and the score tied. He dribbled through a maze of defenders to create space for a jump shot from mid-range.

The ball left his fingertips, lingered in the air, and then, with a soft swish-- landed on the target, securing the Hornets' victory!

Chris Paul finished the game with 43 points, nine assists, four thefts, and five rebounds. But what made this performance truly magical was his ability to control the game's tempo and make clutch shots when it counted.

Even the opponents had to tip their hats to the magician on the court, as the audience erupted in applause. With his spellbinding performance, Chris Paul had not only won the game, but also the respect of fans around the globe.

Chris Paul's extraordinary skill is a prime example of the magic he brings to the basketball court, Young basketball players can look up to Paul as a true wizard of the game, a player whose magic lies not in tactics but in his unwavering commitment to develop his exceptional skills.

CONCLUSION

We have embarked on an incredible journey through the biographies and iconic games of some of the finest NBA players of all time, young readers. As this journey comes to a close, we can learn lessons from these basketball legends that extend far beyond the court.

The stories of these athletes first and foremost teach us the value of perseverance. They persisted regardless of the obstacles they encountered, whether it was overcoming personal calamities, defying expectations, or battling through injuries. They remind us that perseverance, tenacity, and resolve are the pillars of success in any endeavor.

Another important lesson is the value of teamwork. Even the most extraordinary individual talents in the NBA recognize the importance of teamwork, transferring the ball, and supporting teammates. They remind us that while individual brilliance can flourish, it is typically the collective effort of a team that results in victory.

These athletes' stories also illustrate the importance of learning from failure. Each of them experienced career setbacks, but they used them as stepping stones to accomplish greatness. Failure teaches us that it is not the end, but a necessary step on the path to success.

They teach us the importance of unrelenting effort, the strength of self-confidence, resiliency in the face of adversity, and sportsmanship. These tales motivate us to pursue our ambitions, overcome obstacles, and conduct ourselves with honor and dignity. They serve as a reminder that excellence is attainable, whether on the basketball court or along the path of life. The NBA's legends are not only sports heroes, but also beacons of optimism and direction, illuminating the path to our own victories on and off the court.

Lastly, these legendary athletes emphasize the significance of passion and affection for one's work. They played basketball not only as a profession, but also out of a profound and abiding passion for the sport. This compelled them to practice, advance, and pursue excellence.

Remember these legends' words as you pursue your own ambitions, whether in basketball or any other field. Embrace the difficulties, work as a team, learn from your errors, and, above all, be enthusiastic about your journey. The stories of these extraordinary athletes demonstrate that with commitment and passion, anyone can achieve greatness and leave a lasting legacy.

Use these stories as a source of inspiration, youthful readers, whether you're on the court or in the classroom. As you confront life's challenges and pursue your own dreams, remember the sage advice of these NBA legends and incorporate their lessons into your own success story!

Made in United States
Troutdale, OR
01/29/2024

17289408R00075